A-Z RED KIDDE

CONTEN

Key to Map Pages	2-3
Map Pages	4-31
Index to Streets, Towns, Villages and selected Places of Interest	32-40

REFERENCE

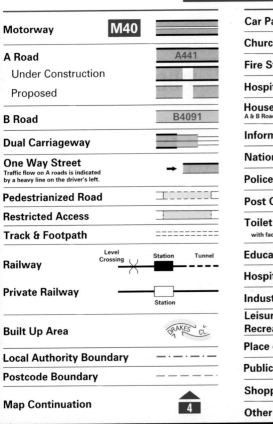

Motorway	**M40**
A Road	A441
Under Construction	
Proposed	
B Road	B4091
Dual Carriageway	
One Way Street Traffic flow on A roads is indicated by a heavy line on the driver's left.	→
Pedestrianized Road	
Restricted Access	
Track & Footpath	
Railway	Level Crossing ╳ Station ■ Tunnel
Private Railway	Station
Built Up Area	DRAKES CL
Local Authority Boundary	
Postcode Boundary	
Map Continuation	4

Car Park	**P**
Church or Chapel	†
Fire Station	■
Hospital	**H**
House Numbers A & B Roads only	22 48
Information Centre	**i**
National Grid Reference	405
Police Station	▲
Post Office	★
Toilet with facilities for the Disabled	▽ ♿
Educational Establishment	◳
Hospital or Health Centre	◳
Industrial Building	◳
Leisure or Recreational Facility	◳
Place of Interest	◳
Public Building	◳
Shopping Centre or Market	◳
Other Selected Buildings	◳

Scale

1:15,840

4 inches (10.16 cm) to 1 mile
6.31cm to 1kilometre

0	¼	½	¾	1 Mile

0	250	500	750 Metres	1 Kilometre

Geographers' A-Z Map Company Limited

Head Office :
Fairfield Road, Borough Green, Sevenoaks, Kent TN15 8PP
Tel: 01732 781000

Showrooms :
44 Gray's Inn Road, London WC1X 8HX
Tel: 020 7440 9500

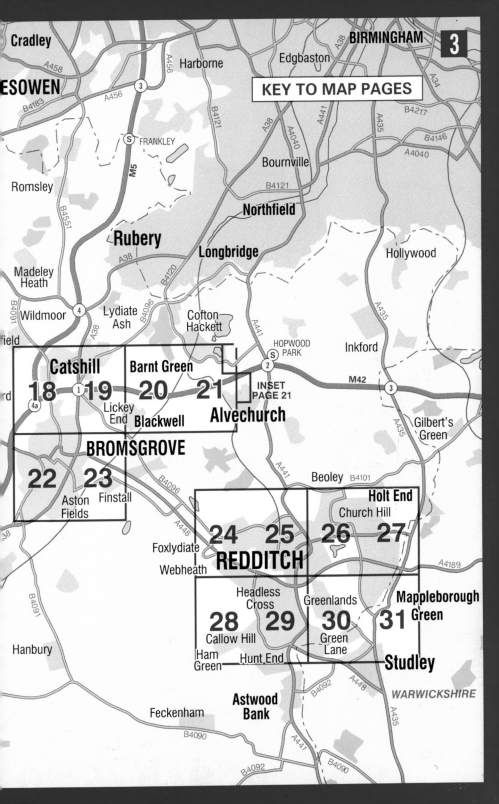

KEY TO MAP PAGES

3

Cradley

ESOWEN

BIRMINGHAM

Harborne

Edgbaston

A458

A456

FRANKLEY

Romsley

M5

Bournville

Northfield

Rubery

Longbridge

Hollywood

Madeley Heath

Cofton Hackett

HOPWOOD PARK

Inkford

Wildmoor

Lydiate Ash

Catshill 18 19 **Barnt Green** 20 21

INSET PAGE 21

M42

Lickey End

Blackwell

Alvechurch

Gilbert's Green

BROMSGROVE

Beoley

Holt End

22 23

Aston Fields

Finstall

24 25 26 27

Church Hill

Foxlydiate

REDDITCH

Webheath

Headless Cross

Greenlands

Mappleborough Green

28 29 30 31

Hanbury

Callow Hill

Green Lane

Ham Green

Hunt End

Studley

Feckenham

Astwood Bank

WARWICKSHIRE

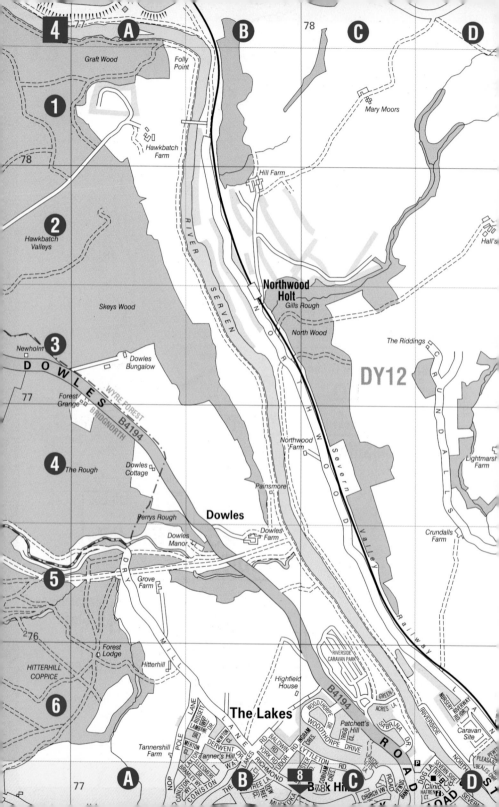

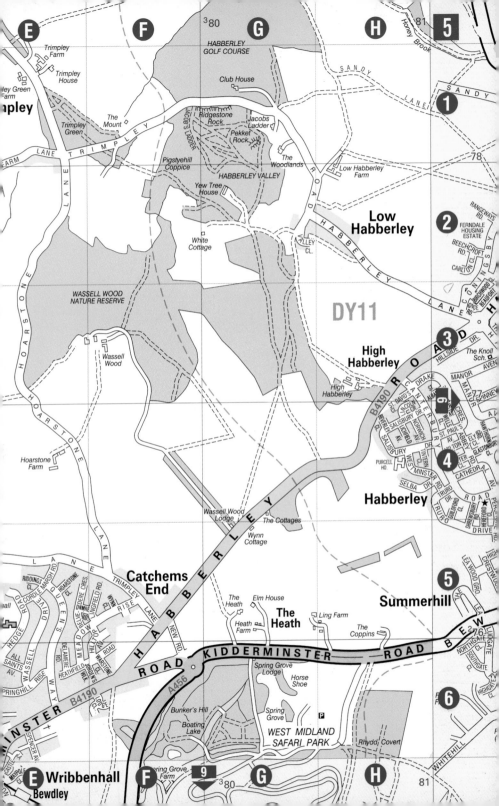

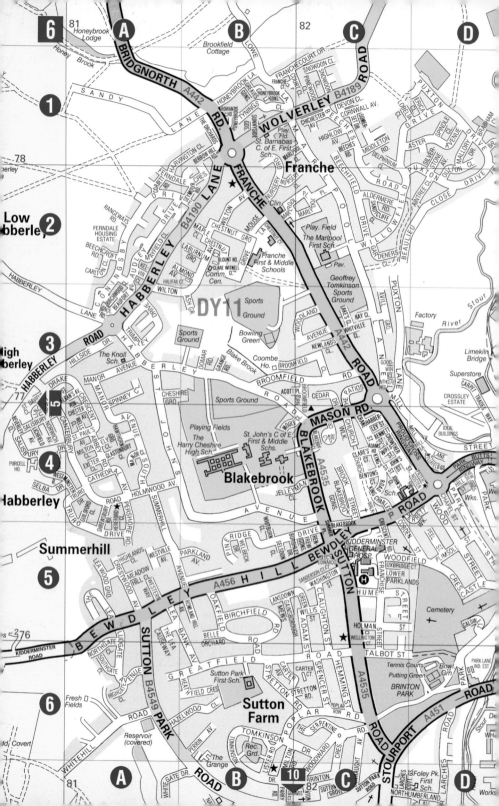

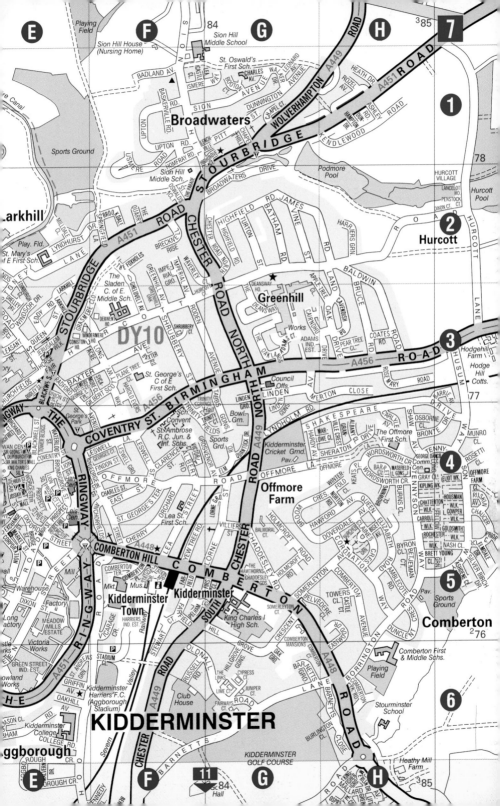

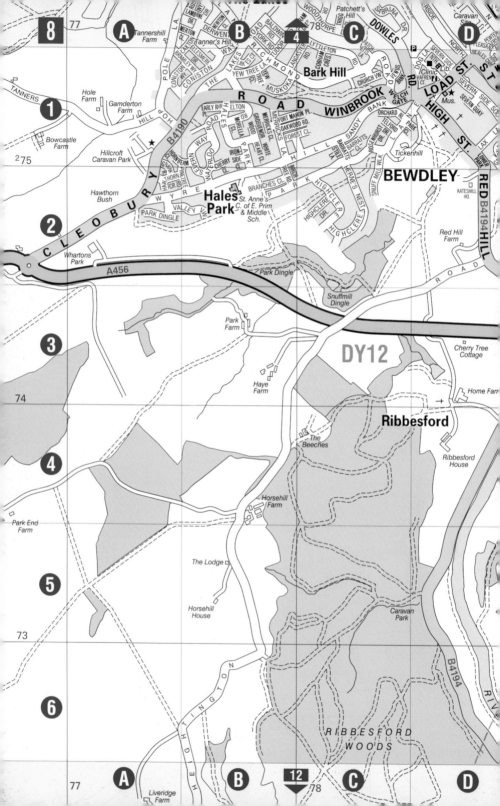

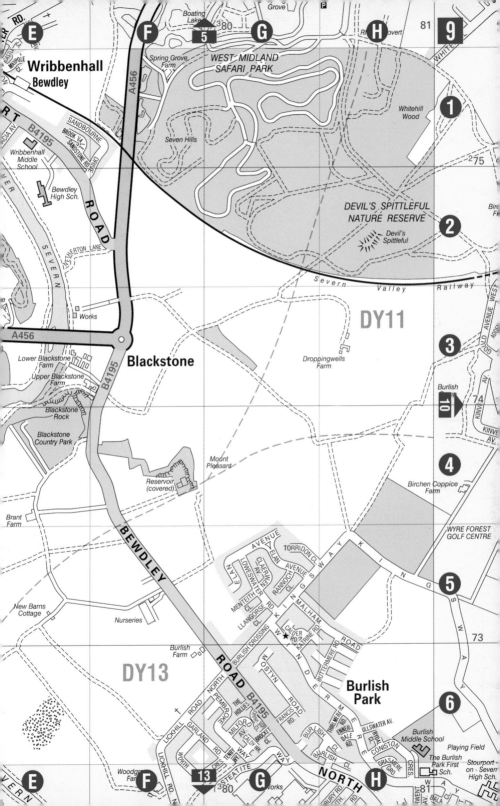

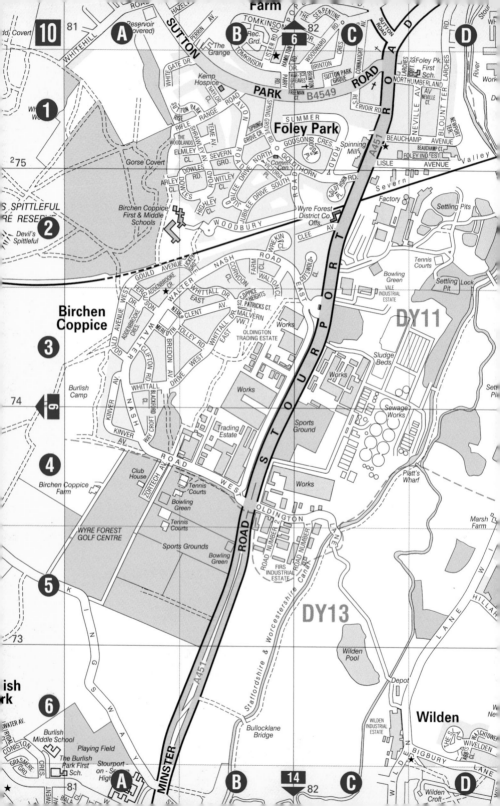

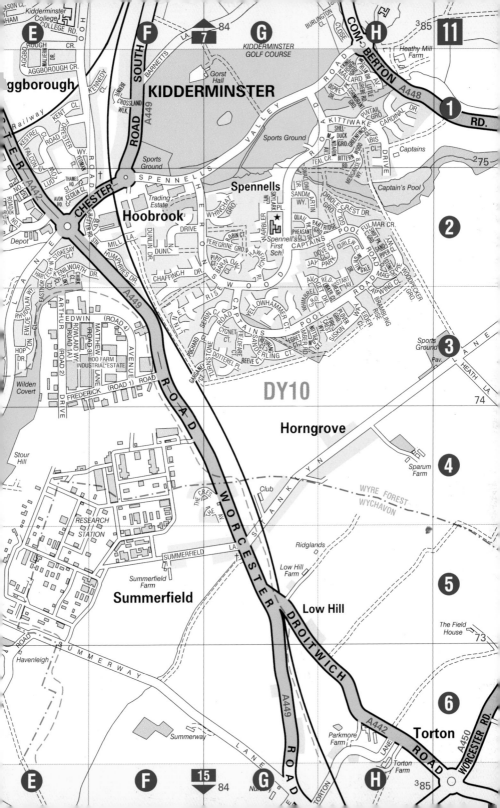

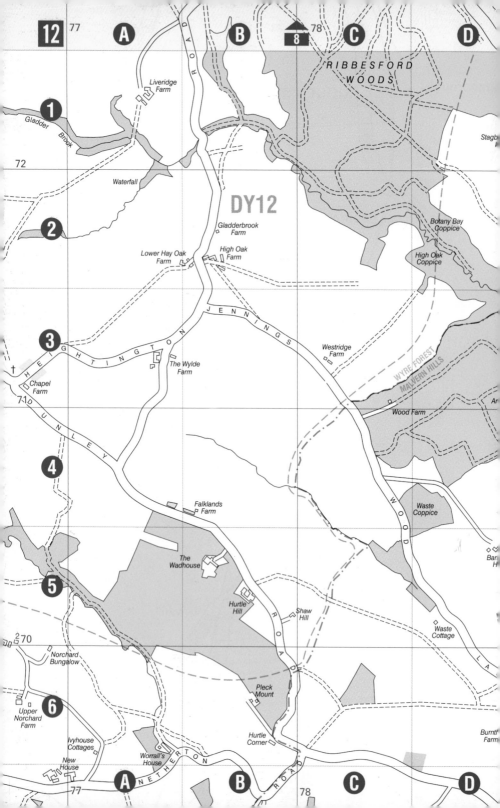

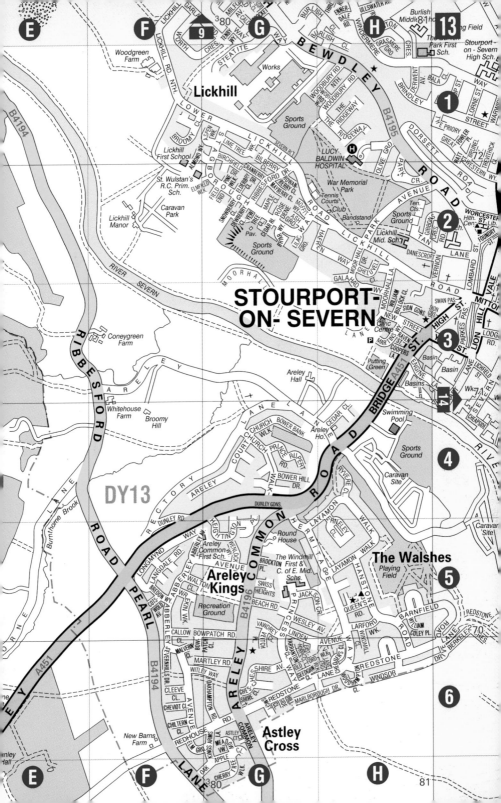

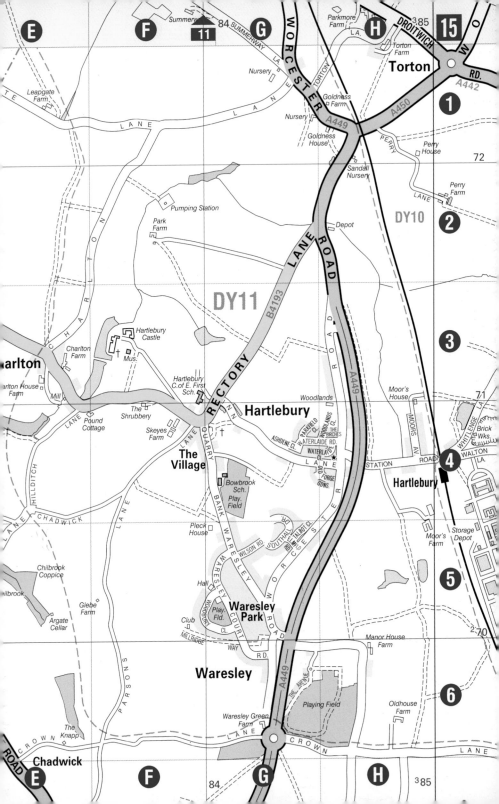

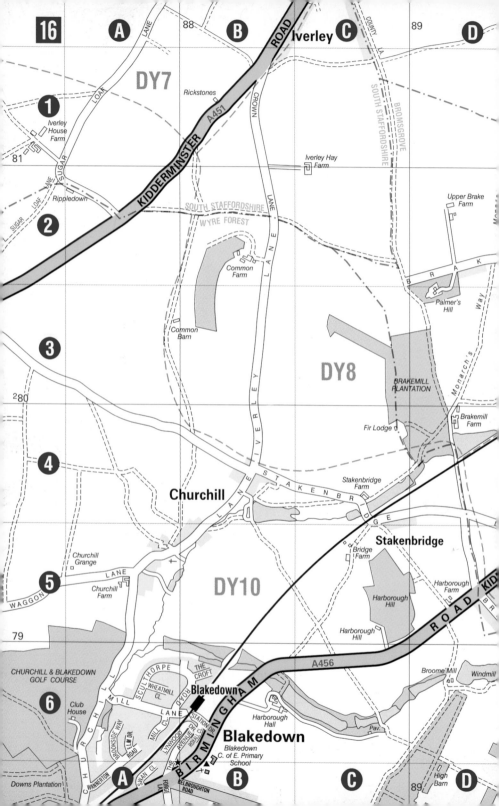

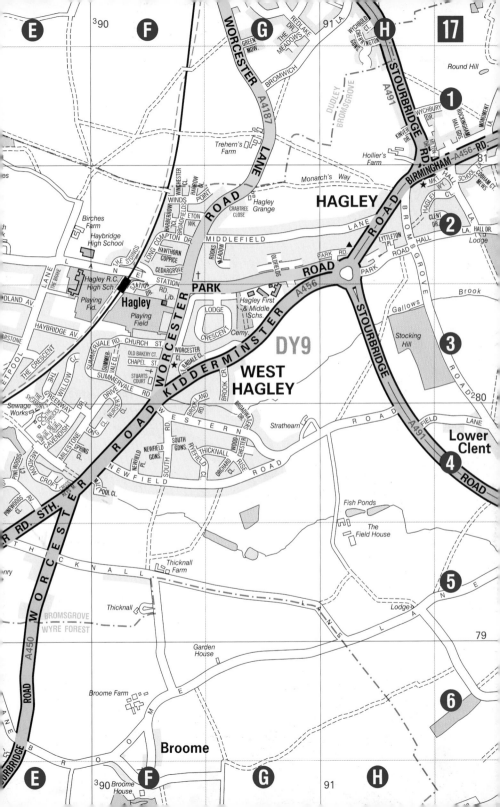

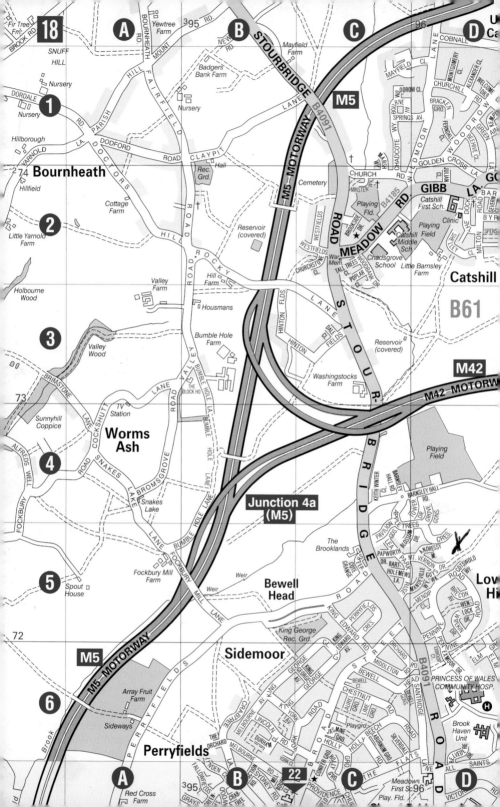

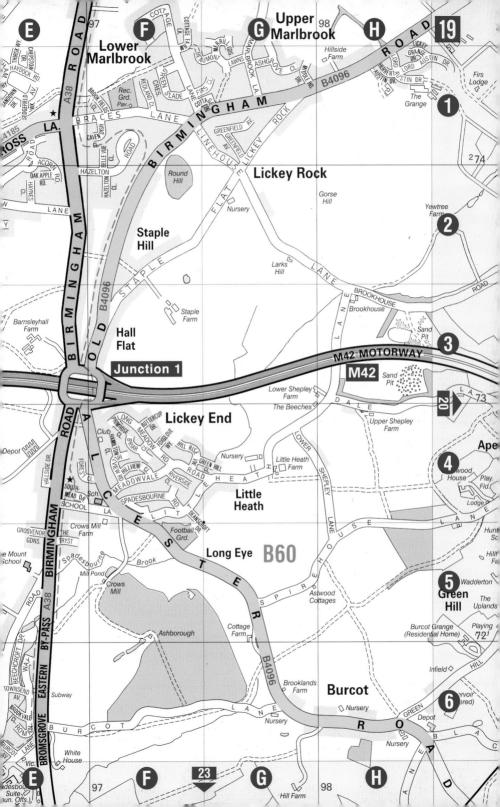

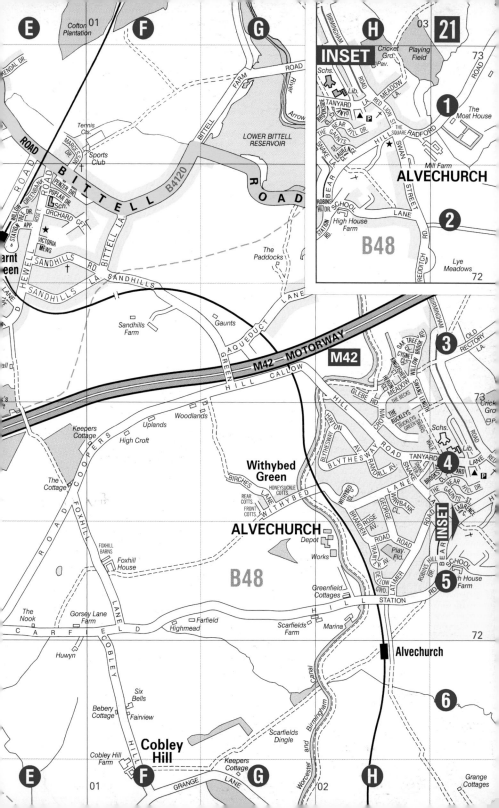

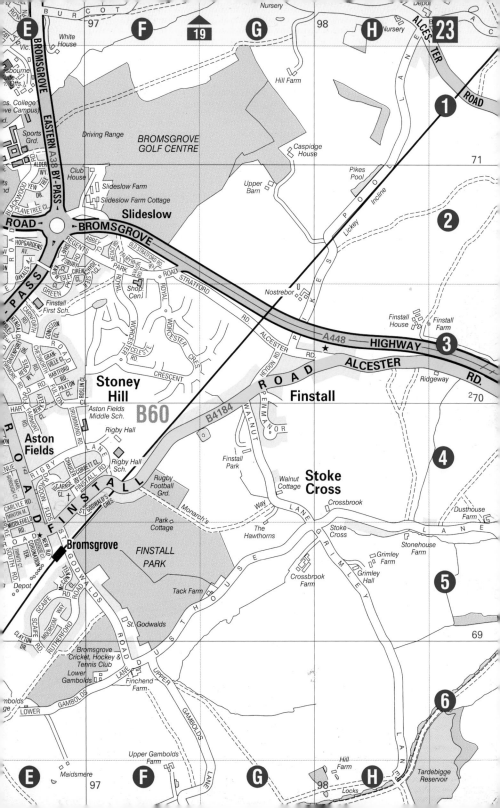

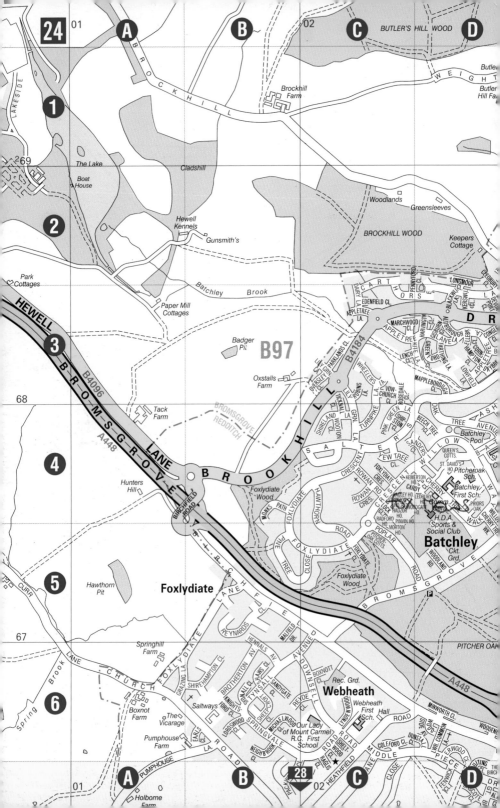

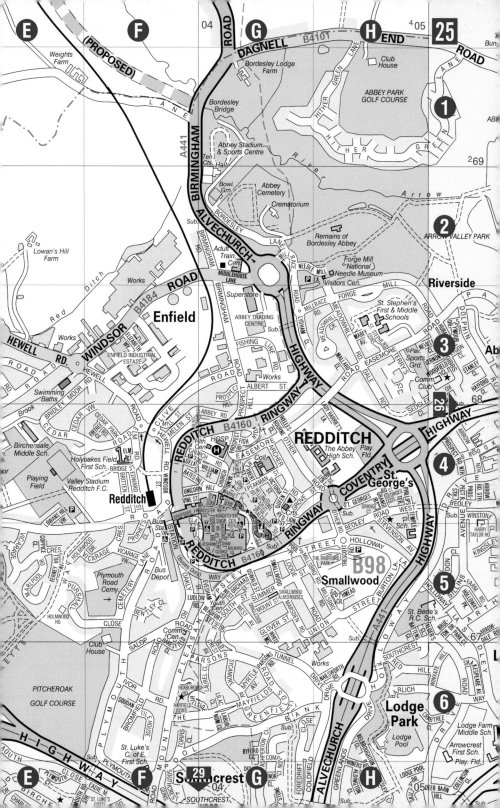

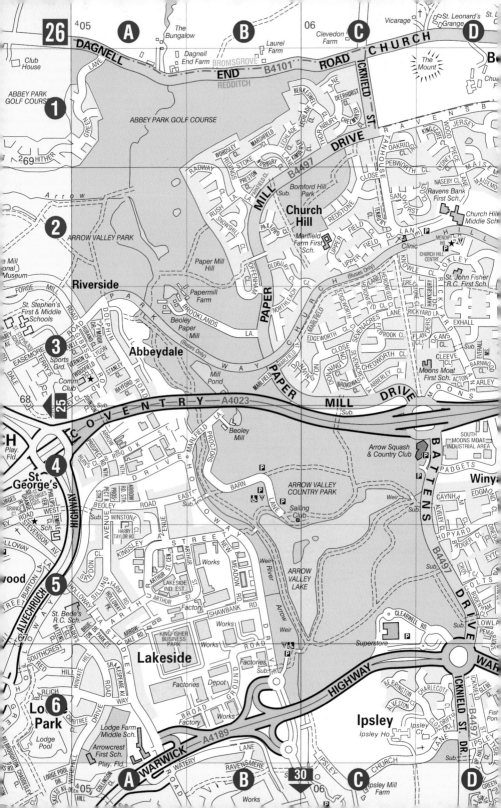

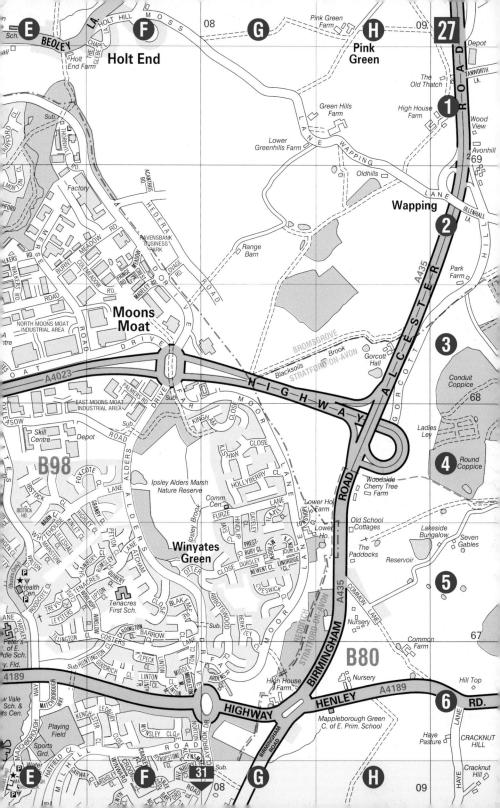

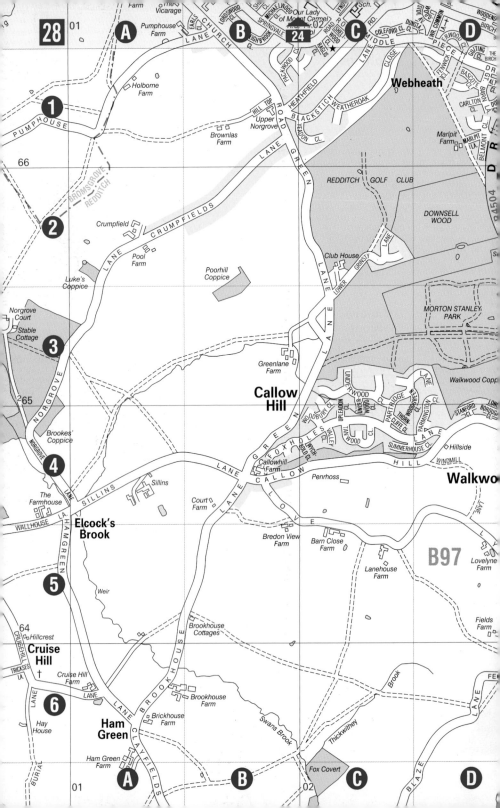

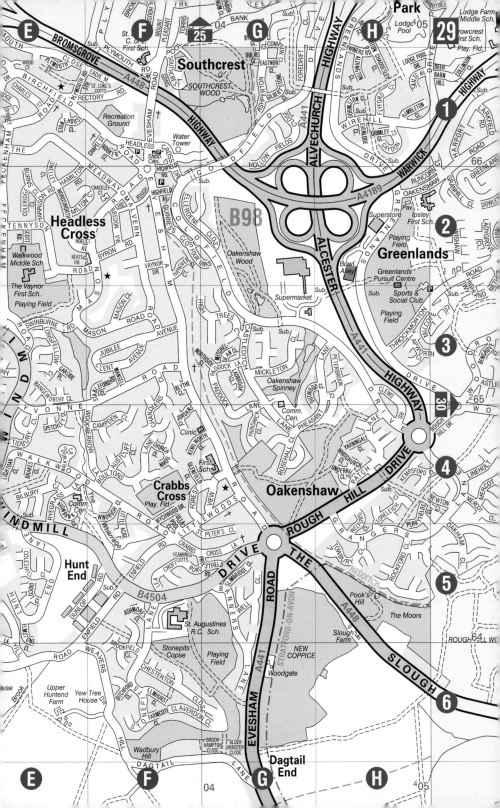

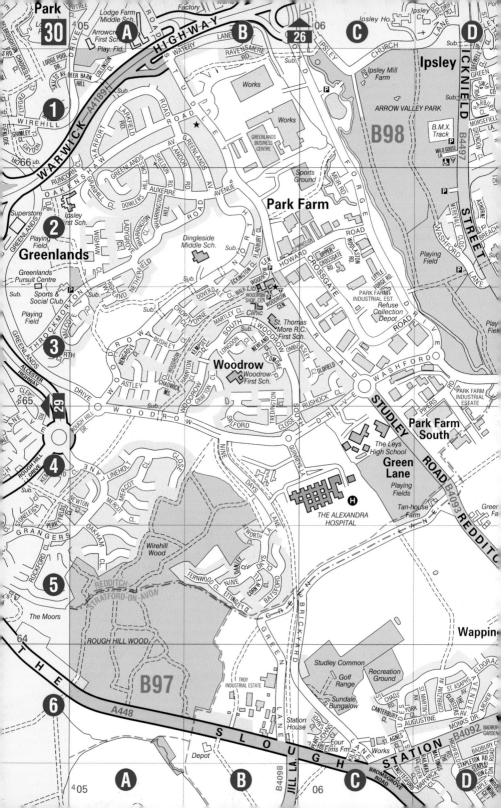

INDEX

Including Streets, Places & Areas, Industrial Estates, Selected Subsidiary Addresses
and Selected Places of Interest.

HOW TO USE THIS INDEX

1. Each street name is followed by its Posttown or Postal Locality and then by its map reference; e.g. Abberley Av. *Stour S* —5F **13** is in the Stourport-on-Severn Posttown and is to be found in square 5F on page **13**. The page number being shown in bold type.
A strict alphabetical order is followed in which Av., Rd., St., etc. (though abbreviated) are read in full and as part of the street name; e.g. Birch Tree Rd. appears after Birchfield Rd. but before Birchwood Clo.

2. Streets and a selection of Subsidiary names not shown on the Maps, appear in the index in *Italics* with the thoroughfare to which it is connected shown in brackets; e.g. *Abberton Ho. Redd —4C 24 (off Lock Clo.)*

3. Places and areas are shown in the index in **bold type**, the map reference referring to the actual map square in which the town or area is located and not to the place name; e.g. **Abbeydale.** —3A **26**

4. An example of a selected place of interest is Arrow Valley Country Pk. —4C **26**

GENERAL ABBREVIATIONS

All : Alley	Cir : Circus	Gt : Great	M : Mews	Sq : Square
App : Approach	Clo : Close	Grn : Green	Mt : Mount	Sta : Station
Arc : Arcade	Comn : Common	Gro : Grove	Mus : Museum	St : Street
Av : Avenue	Cotts : Cottages	Ho : House	N : North	Ter : Terrace
Bk : Back	Ct : Court	Ind : Industrial	Pal : Palace	Trad : Trading
Boulevd : Boulevard	Cres : Crescent	Info : Information	Pde : Parade	Up : Upper
Bri : Bridge	Cft : Croft	Junct : Junction	Pk : Park	Va : Vale
B'way : Broadway	Dri : Drive	La : Lane	Pas : Passage	Vw : View
Bldgs : Buildings	E : East	Lit : Little	Pl : Place	Vs : Villas
Bus : Business	Embkmt : Embankment	Lwr : Lower	Quad : Quadrant	Vis : Visitors
Cvn : Caravan	Est : Estate	Mc : Mac	Res : Residential	Wlk : Walk
Cen : Centre	Fld : Field	Mnr : Manor	Ri : Rise	W : West
Chu : Church	Gdns : Gardens	Mans : Mansions	Rd : Road	Yd : Yard
Chyd : Churchyard	Gth : Garth	Mkt : Market	Shop : Shopping	
Circ : Circle	Ga : Gate	Mdw : Meadow	S : South	

POSTTOWN AND POSTAL LOCALITY ABBREVIATIONS

Agg : Aggborough	*Call H* : Callow Hill	*Head X* : Headless Cross	*Moons M* : Moons Moat North	*Stone* : Stone
A'chu : Alvechurch	*Cats* : Catshill	*H'ton* : Heightington	*Moons I* : Moons Moat North	*Stourb* : Stourbridge
A'wd B : Astwood Bank	*Chu H* : Church Hill North	*H End* : Hunt End	Ind. Est.	*Stour S* : Stourport-on-Severn
B Grn : Barnt Green	*C'hill* : Churchill	*Hurc* : Hurcott	*Park I* : Park Farm Ind. Est.	*Stud* : Studley
Belb : Belbroughton	*Clent* : Clent	*Ips* : Ipsley	*Redd* : Redditch	*Summ* : Summerfield
B'ley : Bentley	*D'frd* : Dodford	*I'ley* : Iverley (Kidderminster)	*Redn* : Rednal	*Tard* : Tardebigge
Beo : Beoley	*Dunl* : Dunley	*Iver* : Iverley (Stourbridge)	*Ribb* : Ribbesford	*Tort* : Torton
Bew : Bewdley	*Elc B* : Elcocks Brook	*Kidd* : Kidderminster	*Shens* : Shenstone	*Trim* : Trimpley
B'wll : Blackwell	*Fair* : Fairfield	*L End* : Lickey End	(Kidderminster)	*Up Ben* : Upper Bentley
Blak : Blakedown	*Fins* : Finstall	*Low H* : Low Habberley	*Shen* : Shenstone (Lichfield)	*U War* : Upton Warren
B'hth : Bournheath	*Hag* : Hagley	*Map G* : Mappleborough	*Side* : Sidemoor	*Ware* : Waresley
B'gve : Bromsgrove	*Ham G* : Ham Green	Green	*Stoke H* : Stoke Heath	*Web* : Webheath
Burc : Burcot	*Hartl* : Hartlebury	*Marl* : Marlbrook	*S Prior* : Stoke Prior	

INDEX

Abberley Av. *Stour S* —5F **13**
Abberley Clo. *Redd* —3C **26**
Abberton Ho. Redd —4C 24
(off Lock Clo.)
Abbeydale. —3A **26**
Abbeyfields Dri. *Stud* —4E **31**
Abbey Clo. *B'gve* —2F **23**
Abbey Rd. *Kidd* —4A **6**
Abbey Rd. *Redd* —4G **25**
Abbey Trad. Cen. *Redd*
—3G **25**
Abbotswood Clo. *Redd*
—5G **27**
Abbotts Clo. *Stour S* —6D **10**
Acacia Av. *Bew* —1E **9**
Acanthus Rd. *Redd* —2F **27**
Acorn Rd. *Cats* —1E **19**
Acorns, The. *Cats* —2D **18**
Acton Clo. *Redd* —3D **26**
Adams Ct. *Kidd* —3G **7**
Adams Ho. *Kidd* —4C **6**
Adam St. *Kidd* —5C **6**
Addenbrooke Cres. *Kidd*
(in two parts) —3A **10**
Adelaide St. *Redd* —4F **25**
Aggborough. —6E **7**
Aggborough Cres. *Kidd*
—1E **11**
Agmore La. *Tard* —6C **20**
Agmore Rd. *B'wll* —6B **20**

Aintree Clo. *Cats* —1D **18**
Aintree Clo. *Kidd* —2D **6**
Albany Clo. *Kidd* —4H **7**
Albert Clo. *Stud* —6E **31**
Albert Rd. *B'gve* —4B **22**
Albert Rd. *Kidd* —4F **7**
Albert St. *Redd* —3G **25**
Albury Rd. *Stud* —6E **31**
Alcester Highway. *Redd*
—2H **29**
Alcester Rd. *Beo* —3H **27**
Alcester Rd. *Fins* —3G **23**
Alcester Rd. *L End & Burc*
—4F **19**
Alcester Rd. *Stud* —6E **31**
Alcester Rd. *Redd* —4G **25**
Aldborough La. *Redd* —3D **24**
Alderbrook Clo. *Redd*
—3D **24**
Alderley Rd. *B'gve* —4A **22**
Aldermans La. *Redd* —2D **24**
Aldermere Rd. *Kidd* —2C **6**
Alderminster Clo. *Redd*
—6G **29**
Alder's Clo. *Redd* —5A **26**
Alders Dri. *Redd* —4F **27**
Alder Way. *B'gve* —2E **23**
Aldington Clo. *Redd* —1H **29**
Alexander Clo. *Cats* —1D **18**
Alfreds Well. *D'frd* —4A **18**
Allensmore Clo. *Redd* —6F **27**

All Saints Av. *Bew* —6E **5**
All Saints Rd. *B'gve* —1D **22**
Almond Av. *Kidd* —2B **6**
Almond Way. *Stour S* —2F **13**
Alton Clo. *Redd* —1D **28**
Alvechurch. —2H **21**
Alvechurch Highway. *Redd*
—2G **25**
Alvechurch Ho. B'gve —1E 23
(off Burcot La.)
Alveley Clo. *Redd* —4D **26**
Alveston Clo. *Redd* —6C **26**
Ambergate Clo. *Redd* —3D **24**
Amblecote Rd. *Kidd* —5H **7**
Ambleside Way. *B'gve*
—3E **23**
Amphlett Ct. *B'gve* —2D **22**
Anchor Fields. *Kidd* —4F **7**
Andressy M. *B'gve* —5D **18**
Ansley Clo. *Redd* —1F **31**
Ansley Clo. *Redd* —2G **25**
Apes Dale. —4A **20**
Apple Tree Clo. *Kidd* —2G **7**
Appletree La. *Redd* —4C **24**
Appletrees Cres. *B'gve*
—4C **18**
Aqueduct La. *A'chu* —3G **21**
Archer Clo. *Stud* —6D **30**
Archer Rd. *Redd* —6G **25**
Arch Hill. *Kidd* —4E **7**
Arden Ho. B'gve —1E 23
(off Burcot La.)

Ardens Clo. *Redd* —6G **27**
Areley Comn. *Stour S*
—6G **13**
Areley Ct. *Stour S* —4F **13**
Areley La. *Stour S* —3F **13**
Areley Kings. —5G **13**
Areley La. *Stour S* —3F **13**
Arley Clo. *Kidd* —2A **10**
Arley Clo. *Redd* —3D **26**
Arrowdale Rd. *Redd* —5A **26**
Arrow Rd. N. *Redd* —4A **26**
Arrow Rd. S. *Redd* —4A **26**
Arrow Valley Country Pk.
—4C **26**
Arthur Dri. *Kidd* —3E **11**
Arthur St. *Redd* —5A **26**
Arthur St. Cen. *Redd* —5A **26**
Arundel Rd. *B'gve* —3E **23**
Ascot Way. *Cats* —1E **19**
Ashdene Clo. *Hartl* —4G **15**
Ashdene Clo. *Kidd* —5H **7**
Ash Dri. *Cats* —1D **18**
Ash Gro. *Kidd* —3B **6**
Ash Gro. *Stour S* —2G **13**
Ashgrove Clo. *Marl* —1G **19**
Ashley Ct. *Redd* —1B **20**
Ashley Rd. *Kidd* —1H **7**
Ashmores Clo. *Redd* —5F **29**
Ashorne Clo. *Redd* —2D **30**
Ashperton Clo. *Redd* —1G **29**
Ashton Clo. *Redd* —1D **28**
Ash Tree Rd. *Redd* —4D **24**

Aspen Wlk. *Stour S* —1G **13**
Aster Av. *Kidd* —1D **6**
Astley Clo. *Redd* —3A **30**
Astley Ct. *Stour S* —6G **13**
Aston Fields. —4E **23**
Aston Fields Trad. Est. *B'gve*
—6D **23**
Aston Rd. *B'gve* —6C **22**
Atcham Clo. *Redd* —5F **27**
Atchenson Clo. *Stud* —6E **31**
Atherstone Clo. *Redd* —1F **31**
Atworth Clo. *Redd* —5B **30**
Audley Dri. *Kidd* —2A **6**
Augustine Av. *Stud* —6C **30**
Austcliff Clo. *Redd* —4F **29**
Austin Rd. *B'gve* —5B **22**
Auxerre Av. *Redd* —2A **30**
Avalon Rd. *B'gve* —2F **23**
Avenbury Clo. *Redd* —1F **31**
Avenue, The. *B'wll* —4B **20**
Avenue, The. *Blak* —6A **16**
Avenue, The. *Redd* —4G **11**
Avenue, The. *Redd* —6G **15**
Avill Gro. *Kidd* —3C **6**
Avocet Dri. *Kidd* —2G **11**
Avonbank Clo. *Redd* —4E **29**
Avon Clo. *B'gve* —6C **22**
Avoncroft Mus. of Buildings.
—6B **22**
Avoncroft Rd. *Stoke H*
—6A **22**

Avon Ho. *Kidd* —2E **11**
Avon Rd. *Kidd* —1B **10**

Badbury Clo. *Stud* —6D **30**
Badbury Gdns. *Stud* —6D **30**
Badger Clo. *Redd* —5D **26**
Badgers, The. *B Grn* —1B **20**
Badger Way. *B'wll* —5C **20**
Badland Av. *Kidd* —1F **7**
Bala Clo. *Stour S* —1A **14**
Baldwin Rd. *Bew* —6B **4**
Baldwin Rd. *Kidd* —2H **7**
Baldwin Rd. *Stour S* —2B **14**
Balmoral Ct. *Kidd* —5H **7**
Banners La. *Redd* —5G **29**
Bant Hill Rd. *B'gve* —3D **22**
Barford Clo. *Redd* —1F **31**
Bark Hill. —1C 8
Barley Cft. *Stoke H* —5A **22**
Barlich Way. *Redd* —6H **25**
Barn Clo. *Stoke H* —6B **22**
Barnetts Clo. *Kidd* —6H **7**
Barnetts Gro. *Kidd* —6G **7**
Barnett's La. *Kidd* —1F **11**
Barnfield Rd. *B'gve* —3B **22**
Barn Owl Clo. *Kidd* —2G **11**
Barnsley Hall Rd. *B'gve*
—4C **18**
Barnsley Rd. *B'gve* —6D **18**
Barnt Green. —2C 20
Barnwood Clo. *Redd* —3E **25**
Barracks Rd. *Stour S* —5C **14**
Barratts Clo. *Bew* —1C **8**
Barratts Stile La. *Bew* —1C **8**
Barrett Clo. *Kidd* —4H **7**
Barrie Av. *Kidd* —3H **7**
Barrow Clo. *Redd* —5F **27**
Bartestree Clo. *Redd* —1F **31**
Bartholemews La. *B'gve*
—5C **18**
Bartleet Rd. *Redd* —3G **31**
Basckerville Rd. *Kidd* —1F **7**
Bascote Clo. *Redd* —1D **28**
Batchley. —4D 24
Batchley Rd. *Redd* —4D **24**
Bates Hill. *Redd* —4F **25**
Batham Rd. *Kidd* —2G **7**
Batsford Clo. *Redd* —5B **30**
Battens Clo. *Redd* —5H **25**
Battens Dri. *Redd* —4D **26**
Baxter Av. *Kidd* —3E **7**
Baxter Gdns. *Kidd* —3F **7**
Beach Rd. *Stour S* —5G **13**
Beales Corner. *Bew* —1D **8**
Bear Hill. *A'chu* —2H **21**
Bear Hill Dri. *A'chu* —1H **21**
Beauchamp Av. *Kidd* —1C **10**
Beauchamp Ct. *Kidd* —1D **10**
Beaufort Av. *Kidd* —3A **6**
Beaufort St. *Redd* —5G **25**
Beaulieu Clo. *Kidd* —2C **6**
Beaumont Lawns. *Marl*
—1F **19**
Becks, The. *A'chu* —3H **21**
Beechcroft Dri. *B'gve* —6E **19**
Beechcroft Rd. *Kidd* —2A **6**
Beeches Rd. *Redd* —1C **6**
Beechfield Clo. *Kidd* —1C **6**
Beech Pk. Dri. *B Grn* —2D **20**
Beech Rd. *B'gve* —6C **18**
Beech Tree Clo. *Redd*
—4D **24**
Beehive Clo. *Cats* —1D **18**
Belbroughton Clo. *Redd*
—6H **25**
Belbroughton Rd. *Blak*
—6B **16**
Belle Orchard. *Kidd* —5B **6**
Bellevue Clo. *Marl* —1F **19**
Bell La. *Stud* —6A **31**
Bell Mead. *Stud* —6E **31**
Belmont Clo. *Redd* —1D **28**
Belvedere Clo. *Kidd* —5G **7**
Belvedere Cres. *Bew* —5E **5**
Belvedere Dri. *B'gve* —6D **18**
Bengrove Clo. *Redd* —3A **30**

Bennett St. *Kidd* —4C **6**
Bentley Clo. *Redd* —5F **25**
Bentons Ct. *Kidd* —4C **6**
Beoley. —1D 26
Beoley La. *Beo* —1E **27**
Beoley Rd. E. *Redd* —4A **26**
Beoley Rd. W. *Redd* —5A **6**
Berkeley Av. *B'gve* —4E **23**
Berkeley Clo. *Redd* —5G **27**
Berkeley Cres. *Stour S*
—6A **14**
Berkeswell Rd. *Redd* —1B **26**
Bernie Crossland Wlk. *Kidd*
—1F **11**
Berrington Clo. *Redd* —6C **26**
Berrow Hill Rd. *Kidd* —1B **6**
Berrow Vw. *B'gve* —5D **22**
Berry Dri. *B Grn* —1B **20**
Betjeman St. *Kidd* —5H **7**
Beverley Dri. *Kidd* —4H **5**
Bewdley. —1D 8
Bewdley Hill. *Kidd* —5A **6**
Bewdley Mus. —1D 8
Bewdley Rd. *Kidd* —5C **6**
Bewdley Rd. *Stour S* —1H **13**
Bewdley Rd. N. *Stour S*
—5F **9**
Bewdley Tourist Info. Cen.
—1D **8**
Bewell Ct. *B'gve* —6C **18**
Bewell Gdns. *B'gve* —6C **18**
Bewell Head. —5B 18
Bewell Head. *B'gve* —6C **18**
Bigbury La. *Stour S* —6D **10**
Bilberry Clo. *Stour S* —1G **13**
Bilbury Clo. *Redd* —4E **29**
Billy La. *B'wll & B Grn*
—3B **20**
Binton Clo. *Redd* —4F **31**
Birchen Coppice. —3H 9
Birchensale Rd. *Redd* —3E **25**
Birches La. *A'chu* —4G **21**
Birches, The. *Hartl* —4H **15**
Birches, The. *Redd* —1D **28**
Birches, The. *Stour S* —3B **14**
Birchfield Ct. *Redd* —6D **24**
Birchfield Dri. *Stour S*
—1G **13**
Birchfield Rd. *Kidd* —5B **6**
Birchfield Rd. *Redd* —4A **24**
Birch Tree Rd. *Bew* —4F **5**
Birchwood Clo. *Kidd* —3A **6**
Birkdale Av. *B'wll* —5B **20**
Birlingham Ho. *B'gve* —1E **23**
(off Burcot La.)
Birmingham Rd. *A'chu*
—1H **21**
Birmingham Rd. *B'gve*
(in two parts) —1D **22**
Birmingham Rd. *Hag* —2H **17**
Birmingham Rd. *L End & Marl*
—5E **19**
Birmingham Rd. *Redd*
—2F **25**
Birmingham Rd. *Stud &*
Map G —5E **31**
Biset Av. *Kidd* —5H **7**
Bishop Hall Cres. *B'gve*
—5B **22**
Bishopstone Clo. *Redd*
—6F **27**
Bishop St. *Stour S* —1H **14**
Bittell Farm Rd. *B Grn & A'chu*
—1G **21**
Bittell La. *B Grn* —2F **21**
Bittell Rd. *B Grn & A'chu*
—2E **21**
Bittern Wood Rd. *Kidd*
—1H **11**
Blackford Clo. *Kidd* —3A **10**
Black Horse La. *Kidd* —4D **6**
Blackmore La. *B'gve* —1D **22**
Blackstitch La. *Redd* —1C **28**
Blackstone. —3F 9
Blackstone Country Pk.
—4E **9**
Blackthorn Ct. *Redd* —1E **31**
Blackwell. —5C 20

Blackwell La. *Redd* —3D **24**
Blackwell Rd. *B'wll & B Grn*
—6A **20**
Blackwell St. *Kidd* —4E **7**
Blackwood Rd. *B'gve* —2E **23**
Blakebrook. —4B 6
Blakebrook. *Kidd* —4C **6**
Blakebrook Clo. *Kidd* —4C **6**
Blakebrook Gdns. *Kidd* —4C **6**
Blakedown. —6B 16
Blakemere Clo. *Redd* —5F **27**
Blake Rd. *Cats* —2E **19**
Blakes Fld. Dri. *B Grn* —1B **20**
Blenheim Cres. *B'gve* —4D **22**
Blossom Dri. *B'gve* —5C **18**
Blount Ho. *Kidd* —2B **6**
Blount Ter. *Kidd* —1D **10**
Blythe Clo. *Redd* —3F **29**
Blythesway. *A'chu* —4H **21**
Bodenham Clo. *Redd* —5D **26**
Booton Ct. *Kidd* —1G **7**
Boot Piece La. *Redd* —3D **24**
Bordesley Abbey
(remains of). —2H **25**
Bordesley Abbey Vis. Cen.
—2H **25**
Bordesley La. *Redd* —2G **25**
Borrington Rd. *Kidd* —6H **7**
Boultons La. *Redd* —4F **29**
Bourne Av. *Cats* —1C **18**
Bournheath. —2A 18
Bournheath Rd. *Fair* —1A **18**
Bower Bank. *Stour S* —4G **13**
Bower Hill Dri. *Stour S*
—4G **13**
Bowmore Rd. *B'gve* —3E **23**
Bowpatch Clo. *Stour S*
—6F **13**
Bowpatch Rd. *Stour S*
—5F **13**
Boxnott Clo. *Redd* —6C **24**
Brabham Clo. *Kidd* —1D **6**
Bracken Gro. *Cats* —1D **18**
Brake, The. *Hag* —2E **17**
Brambles, The. *Cats* —2D **18**
Brambling Ri. *Kidd* —3H **11**
Bramley Way. *Bew* —1A **8**
Branches Clo. *Redd* —5D **26**
Branden Rd. *A'chu* —4H **21**
Breaches La. *Redd* —2D **30**
Break Bk. Rd. *B'gve* —4A **22**
Brecknell Rd. *Kidd* —2F **7**
Brecon Av. *B'gve* —5D **18**
Bredon Av. *Kidd* —3A **10**
Bredon Rd. *B'gve* —5A **22**
Bredon Vw. *Redd* —2F **29**
Bredon Way. *Stour S* —5F **13**
Brett Young Clo. *Kidd* —5H **7**
Briar Clo. *L End* —4F **19**
Briars, The. *Hag* —4F **17**
Briar Way. *Stour S* —2G **13**
Brickyard La. *Stud* —5C **30**
Bridal Rd. *D'frd* —4A **18**
Bridge St. *Kidd* —5E **7**
Bridge St. *Redd* —4F **25**
Bridge St. *Stour S* —4H **13**
Bridgnorth Rd. *Kidd* —1A **6**
Bridley Moor Rd. *Redd*
—4E **25**
Brimstone La. *D'frd* —3A **18**
Brindley St. *Stour S* —1H **14**
Brinklow Rd. *Redd* —2D **30**
Brinton Clo. *Kidd* —1C **10**
Brinton Cres. *Kidd* —1C **10**
Britten St. *Redd* —4F **25**
Broach Rd. *Stour S* —5B **14**
Broadfields. *Hag* —2F **17**
Broad Ground Rd. *Redd*
—6B **26**
Broad Heath Clo. *Redd*
—3E **25**
Broad St. *B'gve* —1B **22**
Broad St. *Kidd* —3F **7**
Broadwas Clo. *Redd* —3C **26**
Broadwaters. —1F 7
Broadwaters Dri. *Hag*
—4G **17**

Broadwaters Dri. *Kidd* —2G **7**
Brocket Clo. *Stour S* —6G **9**
Brockhill La. *Redd* —1A **24**
Brockton Pl. *Stour S* —5G **13**
Bromfield Rd. *Redd* —6F **25**
Bromsgrove. —2C 22
Bromsgrove Eastern By-Pass.
B'gve —6E **19**
Bromsgrove Highway. *B'gve*
—2F **23**
Bromsgrove Highway. *Redd*
—3A **24**
Bromsgrove Mus. —1D 22
Bromsgrove Rd. *D'frd*
—4A **18**
Bromsgrove Rd. *Hag & Clent*
—2H **17**
Bromsgrove Rd. *Redd*
—5C **24**
Bromsgrove Rd. *Stud*
—6C **30**
Bromsgrove St. *Kidd* —6H **7**
Bromsgrove Tourist
Info. Cen. —1D **22**
Bromwich La. *Stourb* —1G **17**
Bronte Dri. *Kidd* —4H **7**
Brook Cres. *Hag* —3G **17**
Brookdale. *Kidd* —2F **7**
Brookfield Clo. *Redd* —6F **29**
Brookfields Clo. *Marl* —1F **19**
Brookhampton Clo. *Redd*
—6G **29**
Brookhill Dri. *Redd* —4B **24**
Brookhouse La. *Ham G &*
Call H —6A **28**
Brookhouse Rd. *B'wll & B Grn*
—3H **19**
Brookland Rd. *Hag* —4F **17**
Brooklands Dri. *Kidd* —1G **11**
Brooklands La. *Redd* —3B **26**
Brook Rd. *B'gve* —3B **22**
Brook Rd. *Fair* —1A **18**
Brookside Clo. *A'chu* —1H **21**
Brookside Dri. *Cats* —2C **18**
Brookside Way. *Blak* —6A **16**
Brook St. *Kidd* —4C **6**
Brook St. *Redd* —4A **26**
Brook Va. *Bew* —1E **9**
Brookvale Clo. *B'gve* —6E **19**
Brookwood Dri. *B Grn*
—2D **20**
Broom Clo. *B'gve* —2E **23**
Broom Cres. *Kidd* —4G **7**
Broome. —6F 17
Broome La. *Blak* —5D **16**
Broomfield Clo. *Kidd* —3B **6**
Broomfield Grn. *Kidd* —3C **6**
Broomfield Rd. *Kidd* —3B **6**
Broomy Clo. *Stour S* —1F **13**
Brotherton Av. *Redd* —6B **24**
Browning Clo. *Kidd* —4H **7**
Bruce Rd. *Kidd* —3H **7**
Brueton Av. *B'gve* —4D **22**
Brueton Dri. *Redd* —5A **26**
Brunel Clo. *Stour S* —1A **14**
Buckfast Clo. *B'gve* —3A **22**
Buckleys Grn. *A'chu* —4H **21**
Buckleys, The. *A'chu* —4H **21**
Bull Ring. *Kidd* —4E **7**
Bullus Rd. *Stour S* —1A **14**
Bumble Hole La. *D'frd*
(in three parts) —3B **18**
Buntsford Hill. *Stoke H*
—6B **22**
Buntsford Pk. Rd. *B'gve*
—6C **22**
Burcher Grn. *Kidd* —5H **7**
Burcot. —6H 19
Burcot Av. *B'gve* —6E **19**
Burcot Ho. *B'gve* —1E **23**
(off Burcot La.)
Burcot La. *B'gve & Burc*
(in two parts) —1E **23**
Burghley Dri. *Kidd* —5B **6**
Burial La. *Ham G* —6A **28**
Burlington Clo. *Kidd* —6G **7**
Burlish Clo. *Stour S* —6G **9**
Burlish Crossing. *Stour S*
—6G **9**

Burlish Park. —6H 9
Burns Clo. *Kidd* —4H **7**
Burns Clo. *Redd* —2E **29**
Burnthorne La. *Dunl* —6D **12**
Burnt Mdw. Rd. *Moons I &*
Redd —2E **27**
Burton La. *Redd* —2E **27**
Bushley Clo. *Redd* —3A **30**
Butler's Hill La. *Redd* —3D **24**
Buttercup Dri. *L End* —4F **19**
Buttermere Rd. *Stour S*
—6H **9**
Byford Clo. *Redd* —6G **25**
Byland Clo. *B'gve* —3B **22**
Byron Clo. *Kidd* —5H **7**
Byron Rd. *Redd* —2F **29**
Byron Way. *Cats* —2D **18**

Cairndale Dri. *Kidd* —3G **7**
Calder Rd. *Stour S* —5G **9**
Caldwall Cres. *Kidd* —5D **6**
Caldy Wlk. *Stour S* —5G **9**
Callow Hill. —4C 28
Callow Hill. *Call H* —4B **28**
Callow Hill Rd. *A'chu* —3G **21**
Callows La. *Kidd* —4E **7**
Campden Clo. *Redd* —4F **29**
Canalside. *Stour S* —2B **14**
Canterbury Clo. *Stud* —6C **30**
Canterbury Rd. *Kidd* —3H **5**
Captain's Pool Rd. *Kidd*
—2G **11**
Cardinal Cres. *B'gve* —3A **22**
Cardinal Dri. *Kidd* —1H **11**
Cardington Clo. *Redd* —5F **27**
Cardy Rd. *Redd* —4C **24**
Carlton Clo. *Kidd* —2A **6**
Carlton Clo. *Redd* —1D **28**
Carlyle Av. *Kidd* —4H **7**
Carlyle Rd. *B'gve* —4E **23**
Carnforth Rd. *B'gve* —3E **23**
Carnoustie Clo. *B'gve*
—4A **22**
Carol Av. *B'gve* —1A **22**
Carpet Trades Way. *Kidd*
—3D **6**
Carroll Wlk. *Kidd* —6B **6**
Carter Av. *Kidd* —6B **6**
Carter Ct. *Kidd* —6C **6**
Carters Clo. *B'gve* —5A **22**
Carthorse La. *Redd* —3C **24**
Castleditch La. *Redd* —3G **29**
Castle La. *Bew* —1E **9**
Castle Rd. *Kidd* —5D **6**
Castle Rd. *Stud* —6E **31**
Catchems End. —5F 5
Cathedral Av. *Kidd* —4A **6**
Catherine Clo. *B'gve* —4C **22**
Catshill. —2D 18
Cavendish Clo. *Marl* —1F **19**
Cavendish Dri. *Hag* —4E **17**
Cavendish Rd. *Kidd* —3H **7**
Caynham Clo. *Redd* —4D **26**
Cedar Clo. *Stour S* —4H **13**
Cedar Cres. *Kidd* —4C **6**
Cedar Dri. *B'gve* —3D **22**
Cedar Dri. *Kidd* —3C **6**
Cedar Pk. Rd. *Redd* —4F **25**
Cedar Ri. *Stour S* —2G **13**
Cedar Rd. *Redd* —4E **25**
Cedar Ter. *B'gve* —3D **22**
Cedar Vw. *Redd* —4E **25**
Celeste Rd. *B'gve* —2F **23**
Cemetery La. *Redd* —5F **25**
Central Rd. *B'gve* —3D **22**
Chaceley Ct. *Redd* —2F **29**
Chadcote Way. *Cats* —1C **18**
Chaddesley Clo. *Redd*
—1H **29**
Chaddesley Gdns. *Kidd*
—5G **7**
Chaddesley Rd. *Kidd* —5G **7**
Chadwick Bank Ind. Est.
Stour S —6D **14**
Chadwick La. *Stour S & Hartl*
(in two parts) —6D **14**

Chadwick M. *Redd* —3A **30**
Chaffinch Dri. *Kidd* —2F **11**
Chandlers Clo. *Redd* —4F **29**
Chapel Ct. *Kidd* —1G **7**
Chapel Hill. *Kidd* —1G **7**
Chapel La. *Beo* —1F **27**
Chapel St. *B'gve* —2D **22**
Chapel St. *Hag* —3F **17**
Chapel St. *Head X* —1F **29**
Chapel St. *Kidd* —4D **6**
Chapel St. Precinct. *B'gve*
—2D **22**
Chapel Wlk. *B'gve* —2D **22**
Charford. —4C 22
Charford Rd. *B'gve* —4B **22**
Charlecote Clo. *Redd* —6D **26**
Charles Av. *Kidd* —1G **7**
Charles St. *Kidd* —4F **7**
Charles St. *Redd* —1E **29**
Charlton. —3E 15
Charlton La. *Hartl* —3E **15**
Chatterton Wlk. *Kidd* —4H **7**
Chaucer Cres. *Kidd* —4H **7**
Chaucer Rd. *B'gve* —4E **23**
Cheapside. *Stour S* —4A **14**
Chedworth Clo. *Redd* —3C **26**
Chelmarsh Clo. *Redd* —1C **26**
Cheltenham Av. *Cats* —1E **19**
Chepstow Dri. *Cats* —1E **19**
Chequers Clo. *Stour S*
—6H **13**
Cherington Clo. *Redd* —1F **31**
Cherrington Gdns. *Stourb*
—1H **17**
Cherry Clo. *Bew* —1B **8**
Cherry Cres. *B'gve* —2B **22**
Cherry Hill Av. *B Grn* —2D **20**
Cherry Hill Dri. *B Grn* —2D **20**
Cherry Hill Rd. *B Grn* —2D **20**
Cherry Orchard. *Kidd* —5F **7**
Cherry Orchard Dri. *B'gve*
—1B **22**
Cherry Tree Wlk. *Redd*
—4D **24**
Cherry Tree Wlk. *Stour S*
—6G **13**
Cheshire Gro. *Kidd* —3A **6**
Chesshire Av. *Stour S* —6G **13**
Chesshire Clo. *Stour S*
—6G **13**
Chester Rd. N. *Kidd* —2F **7**
Chester Rd. S. *Kidd* —2E **11**
Chesterton Clo. *Redd* —6F **29**
Chestnut Clo. *Redd* —2B **6**
Chestnut Gro. *Kidd* —2B **6**
Chestnut Rd. *B'gve* —6C **18**
Cheswick Clo. *Redd* —5G **27**
Chesworth Rd. *B'gve* —3E **23**
Cheviot Clo. *Stour S* —6F **13**
Chichester Av. *Kidd* —1C **6**
Chiltern Clo. *Stour S* —6F **13**
Chiltern Ho. *Redd* —1E **31**
Chirk Clo. *Kidd* —2E **11**
Church Av. *Stour S* —2A **14**
Church Clo. *B'gve* —2C **22**
Chu. Down Clo. *Redd* —4F **29**
Church Dri. *Stour S* —2A **14**
Churchfields. —1C 22
Churchfields. *B'gve* —1C **22**
Churchfields. *Kidd* —3E **7**
Churchfields Clo. *B'gve*
—1C **22**
Churchfields Gdns. *B'gve*
—1C **22**
Churchfields Rd. *B'gve*
—1C **22**
Church Grn. E. *Redd* —4G **25**
Church Grn. W. *Redd* —4G **25**
Church Hill. —2C 26
Church Hill. *Beo* —1C **26**
Chu. Hill Cen. *Redd* —2D **26**
Chu. Hill Way. *Redd* —3B **26**
Churchill. —4B 16
Churchill La. *Blak* —6A **16**
Churchill Rd. *Cats* —1D **18**
Church La. *B'gve* —2C **22**
Church Rd. *B'gve* —1C **22**
Church Rd. *Cats* —2C **18**
Church Rd. *Redd* —6A **24**

Church Rd. *Redd & Web*
—4F **25**
Churchstone Clo. *Cats*
—2C **18**
Church St. *B'gve* —2C **22**
Church St. *Hag* —3F **17**
Church St. *Kidd* —4E **7**
Church St. *Stud* —6E **31**
Church Vw. *Bew* —1C **8**
Church Wlk. *Kidd* —4C **6**
Church Wlk. *Stour S* —4G **13**
Cirencester Clo. *B'gve* —2E **23**
*Cladsworth Ho. Redd —4C 24
(off Lock Clo.)*
Claerwen Av. *Stour S* —5G **9**
Claines Cres. *Kidd* —5H **7**
Clarence St. *Kidd* —4F **7**
Clarence Way. *Bew* —6D **4**
Clarendon Clo. *Redd* —3D **24**
Clare's Ct. *Kidd* —4C **6**
Clare Witnell Clo. *Kidd* —2B **6**
Clarke St. *Redd* —4F **25**
Claughton St. *Kidd* —5C **6**
Claverdon Clo. *Redd* —6F **29**
Claybrook Dri. *Redd* —3E **31**
Clayfields. *Ham G* —6A **28**
Claypit La. *B'hth* —1B **18**
Clayton Dri. *B'gve* —5E **23**
Clearwell Rd. *Redd* —5C **26**
Clee Av. *Kidd* —2C **10**
Cleeve Clo. *Redd* —3D **26**
Cleeve Clo. *Stour S* —6F **13**
Clensmore St. *Kidd* —3D **6**
Clent Av. *Redd* —3B **10**
Clent Av. *Redd* —3F **29**
Clent Dri. *Hag* —2H **17**
*Clent Ho. B'gve —1E 23
(off Burcot La.)*
Cleobury Clo. *Redd* —2D **24**
Cleobury Rd. *Bew* —2A **8**
Clews Rd. *Redd* —3H **29**
Clifton Clo. *Redd* —1D **30**
Clifton Rd. *Kidd* —3A **10**
Clive Rd. *B'gve* —4E **23**
Clive Rd. *Redd* —4F **25**
Clock Ho., The. *B'hth* —3B **18**
Cloisters, The. *Stud* —6D **30**
Coates Rd. *Redd* —3H **7**
Cobden St. *Kidd* —4C **6**
Cobham Clo. *B'gve* —5C **22**
Cobham Ct. M. *Hag* —2H **17**
Cobham Cres. *Bew* —1C **8**
Cobham Rd. *Kidd* —6E **7**
Cobley Hill. —6F 21
Cobley Hill. *A'chu* —6F **21**
Cobnall Rd. *Cats* —1D **18**
Cockshutt La. *D'frd* —4A **18**
Coldfield Dri. *Redd* —2F **29**
Coleford Clo. *Redd* —6C **24**
Colemeadow Rd. *Moons I*
—2E **27**
Coleridge Clo. *Redd* —2E **29**
Coleshill Clo. *Redd* —5E **29**
College Rd. *B'gve* —2D **22**
College Rd. *Kidd* —6E **7**
College Wlk. *B'gve* —2D **22**
(in two parts)
Collinson Clo. *Redd* —1A **30**
Collis Clo. *B'gve* —5B **22**
Colts La. *Redd* —5D **26**
Comberton. —5H 7
Comberton Av. *Kidd* —5H **7**
Comberton Ct. *Kidd* —6G **7**
Comberton Hill. *Kidd* —5F **7**
Comberton Mans. *Kidd*
—5G **7**
Comberton Pk. Rd. *Kidd*
—6H **7**
Comberton Pl. *Kidd* —5F **7**
Comberton Rd. *Kidd* —5F **7**
Comberton Ter. *Kidd* —5F **7**
Common La. *Map G* —5H **27**
Compton Clo. *Redd* —6G **25**
Congleton Clo. *Redd* —3D **24**
Conifer Gro. *B'gve* —1C **22**
Coningsby Dri. *Kidd* —3A **6**
Coniston Clo. *B'gve* —3E **23**
Coniston Cres. *Stour S*
—6H **9**

Coniston Ho. *Kidd* —3E **7**
Coniston Way. *Bew* —1A **8**
Connaught Av. *Kidd* —1C **10**
Conway Rd. *B'gve* —3C **22**
Cooper Clo. *B'gve* —6B **22**
Coopers Hill. *A'chu* —4E **21**
Coopers La. *Stour S* —3H **13**
Coppice Clo. *Redd* —2A **6**
Coppice Heights. *Redd*
—3B **10**
Corbett Clo. *B'gve* —4E **23**
Corbett Rd. *Kidd* —2A **6**
Corbizum Av. *Stud* —6D **30**
Cordle Marsh Rd. *Bew* —5E **5**
Cormorant Gro. *Kidd* —1H **11**
Corndon Clo. *Kidd* —2B **10**
Cornfield Av. *Stoke H* —6A **22**
Cornhampton Clo. *Redd*
—3D **24**
Cornwall Av. *Kidd* —1C **6**
Cornwell Clo. *Redd* —5B **30**
Coronation Ter. *B'gve* —5E **23**
Coronation Way. *Kidd* —5H **7**
Corporation St. *Kidd* —5E **7**
Cosford Clo. *Redd* —1F **31**
Costers La. *Redd* —5F **27**
Cotswold Av. *Stour S* —5F **13**
Cotswold Clo. *Redd* —2C **10**
Cotswold Way. *B'gve* —5D **18**
Cottage Dri. *Marl* —1F **19**
Cottage Farm La. *Marl* —1F **19**
Cottage La. *Marl* —1F **19**
Cotton Pool Rd. *B'gve*
—2B **22**
Counting Ho. Way. *Stoke H*
—6B **22**
County La. *Iver* —1C **16**
Court Clo. *Kidd* —1B **6**
Coventry Highway. *Redd*
—4H **25**
Coventry St. *Kidd* —4E **7**
Covers, The. *Stud* —4E **31**
Cowper Wlk. *Kidd* —4H **7**
Crabbs Cross. —4F 29
Crabbs Cross La. *Redd*
—5F **29**
Crane St. *Kidd* —4C **6**
Cranham Clo. *Redd* —2D **28**
Crendon Clo. *Stud* —5E **31**
Crescent Rd. *Kidd* —4C **6**
Crescent, The. *B'gve* —3C **22**
Crescent, The. *Hag* —3E **17**
Crescent, The. *Kidd* —4F **11**
Crest Pk. *Redd* —2F **27**
Crestwood Av. *Kidd* —5A **6**
Croft Clo. *Redd* —5D **26**
Croft, The. *Blak* —6B **16**
Crooks La. *Stud* —6D **30**
Croome Clo. *Redd* —1F **31**
Cropthorne Clo. *Redd*
—3A **30**
*Cropthorne Ho. B'gve —1E 23
(off Burcot La.)*
Crossgate Rd. *Park I & Redd*
—2C **30**
Cross Keys M. *Hag* —4E **17**
Crossley Est. *Kidd* —3D **6**
Crossley Wlk. *B'gve* —5B **22**
Crown Clo. *B'gve* —2C **22**
Crown La. *Iver* —1B **16**
Crown La. *Stour S* —6E **15**
Crown La. *Ware* —4E **7**
Crown Mdw. *A'chu* —4H **21**
Crowther St. *Kidd* —4C **6**
Cruisehill La. *Ham G* —5A **28**
Crumpfields La. *Redd* —2A **28**
Crundalls La. *Bew* —3D **4**
Curlew Clo. *Kidd* —2F **11**
Curr La. *Up Ben* —5A **24**
Cutty Sark Dri. *Stour S*
—4B **14**

Cygnet Clo. *A'chu* —3H **21**
Cygnet Ct. *Kidd* —3G **11**
Cypress Ct. *Kidd* —6G **7**

Dagnell End Rd. *Redd*
—1G **25**
Dagtail End. —6G 29
Dagtail La. *Redd* —6F **29**
Dairy La. *Redd* —3C **24**
Dale Clo. *B'hth* —3C **18**
Dale Hill. *B'wll* —4A **20**
Dale La. *L End* —3H **19**
Dale Rd. *Redd* —3H **25**
Damson Clo. *Call H* —4E **29**
Damson Way. *Bew* —6E **5**
Danescroft. *Stour S* —2H **13**
Danzey Clo. *Redd* —5B **30**
Dark La. *Stoke H* —6A **22**
Davenport Dri. *B'gve* —3E **23**
Dawson Rd. *B'gve* —2A **22**
Daybrook Clo. *Redd* —3D **24**
Deans Clo. *Redd* —3D **26**
Deanscroft Dri. *L End* —4F **19**
Deansway. *B'gve* —3A **22**
Deansway Ho. *Redd* —2G **7**
Deansway, The. *Redd* —3G **7**
Deer Barn Hill. *Redd* —1A **30**
Deerhurst Clo. *Redd* —1C **26**
Delamere Rd. *Bew* —6E **5**
Dellow Gro. *A'chu* —5H **21**
Delphinium Clo. *Kidd* —1H **11**
Denehurst Clo. *B Grn* —1B **20**
Derick Burcher's Mall. *Kidd*
—4E **7**
Derwent Av. *Stour S* —1H **13**
Derwent Dri. *Bew* —6B **4**
Derwent Ho. *Redd* —3F **7**
Derwent Way. *B'gve* —3E **23**
**Devil's Spittleful & Rifle
Range Nature Reserve.**
—2H **9**
Devon Clo. *Kidd* —1C **6**
Devonport Clo. *Redd* —3D **24**
Dewberry Clo. *Stour S*
—2G **13**
Didcot Clo. *Redd* —5E **29**
Dilwyn Clo. *Redd* —1F **31**
Dinedor Clo. *Redd* —5D **26**
Dingleside. *Redd* —5G **25**
Dinmore Clo. *Redd* —5D **26**
Discovery Rd. *Stour S*
—4B **14**
Ditchford Clo. *Redd* —6F **29**
Dixon Ct. *Kidd* —2H **7**
Dixon St. *Kidd* —5E **7**
Dock, The. *Cats* —2D **18**
Doctors Hill. *B'hth* —1A **18**
*Dodford Ho. B'gve —1E 23
(off Burcot La.)*
Dodford Rd. *B'hth* —1A **18**
Dog La. *Bew* —1D **8**
Dolben La. *Redd* —5D **26**
Dolphin Rd. *Redd* —3A **26**
Domar Rd. *Redd* —3B **6**
Donnington Clo. *Redd*
—3B **26**
Dordale Rd. *B'hth* —1A **18**
Dormston Clo. *Redd* —1H **29**
Dorridge Clo. *Redd* —1D **28**
Dorsett Rd. *Stour S* —1H **13**
Dotterel Pl. *Kidd* —3G **11**
Dove Clo. *Kidd* —2H **11**
Dovecote Rd. *B'gve* —3B **22**
Doverdale Av. *Kidd* —5H **7**
Doverdale Clo. *Redd* —3B **30**
Dowlers Hill Cres. *Redd*
—2A **30**
Dowles Rd. *Bew* —3A **4**
Dowles Rd. *Kidd* —2B **10**
Downsell Rd. *Redd* —6C **24**
Dragoon Fields. *B'gve* —4E **23**
Drake Cres. *Kidd* —3H **5**
Drakes Clo. *Redd* —4E **29**
Draycott Clo. *Redd* —3E **25**
Drayton Clo. *Redd* —2D **30**
Drayton Ct. *B'gve* —4E **23**
Driffield Clo. *Redd* —6D **26**
Drive, The. *Redd* —5G **25**

Droitwich Rd. *Tort* —5G **11**
Drovers Way. *B'gve* —6B **22**
Drummond Rd. *B'gve* —4E **23**
Dry Mill La. *Bew* —5A **4**
Dudley St. *Kidd* —4D **6**
Dulais Clo. *Redd* —1G **29**
Dunchurch Clo. *Redd* —1F **31**
Dunclent Cres. *Redd* —5H **7**
Dunedin Dri. *B Grn* —1C **20**
Dunhampton Dri. *Redd* —1H **7**
Dunley Gdns. *Stour S* —4G **13**
Dunley Rd. *H'ton* —3A **12**
Dunley Rd. *Stour S* —6D **12**
Dunlin Dri. *Kidd* —2F **11**
Dunlop Rd. *Redd* —5E **29**
Dunmore Rd. *Bew* —5E **5**
Dunnington Av. *Kidd* —1G **7**
Dunstall Clo. *Redd* —6D **24**
Durham Clo. *B'gve* —6B **18**
Dursley La. *Redd* —5G **27**
Dusthouse La. *Fins* —6F **23**
Duxford Clo. *Redd* —2D **28**

Eadie M. *Redd* —1F **29**
Eagle Rd. *Moons M* —3E **27**
Eardisley Clo. *Redd* —1F **31**
Earls Clo. *Redd* —6B **24**
Early River Pl. *Bew* —1B **8**
Easemore Rd. *Redd* —4G **25**
Easenhall La. *Redd* —1E **31**
Easthorpe Clo. *Stour S*
—6G **13**
E. Moons Moat Ind. Area.
Redd —3E **27**
Eastnor Clo. *Redd* —3E **11**
Eastnor Clo. *Redd* —1G **29**
East Rd. *B'gve* —3D **22**
East Rd. *Stour S* —1A **14**
East St. *Kidd* —4F **7**
Eastwood Dri. *Redd* —6H **7**
Eathorpe Clo. *Redd* —2E **31**
Echells Clo. *B'gve* —2A **22**
Eckington Clo. *Redd* —2B **30**
Eddy Rd. *Kidd* —3E **7**
Eden Clo. *Stud* —6D **30**
Edenfield Clo. *Redd* —3C **30**
Edgewood Dri. *B Grn* —1C **20**
(in two parts)
Edgeworth Clo. *Redd* —3C **26**
Edgmond Clo. *Redd* —4D **26**
Edinburgh Clo. *Redd* —3E **7**
Ednall La. *B'gve* —2D **22**
Edward St. *Redd* —4F **25**
Edwin Av. *Kidd* —2F **7**
Edwin Ct. *B'gve* —4C **22**
Edwin Cres. *B'gve* —4C **22**
Egret Ct. *Kidd* —3G **11**
Eider Clo. *Kidd* —3H **11**
Elan Av. *Stour S* —5G **9**
Elderberry Clo. *Stour S*
—2G **13**
Eldersfield Clo. *Redd* —1E **27**
Eldorado Clo. *Stud* —6D **30**
Elgar M. *B'gve* —2C **22**
Eliot Wlk. *Kidd* —4H **7**
Elizabeth Way. *Redd* —3F **25**
Ellenbrook Clo. *Redd* —3D **24**
Ellerdene Clo. *Redd* —2F **29**
Ellesmere Dri. *Bew* —1B **8**
Ellis Gro. *Hag* —4F **17**
Elm Ct. *Redd* —4F **25**
Elmdale Dri. *Redd* —5H **7**
Elm Dri. *Blak* —6A **16**
Elmfield Rd. *Hartl* —5G **15**
Elmfield Wlk. *Stour S* —2F **13**
Elm Gro. *B'gve* —6D **18**
Elm Gro. *Stour S* —6F **13**
Elmhurst Clo. *Redd* —6F **29**
Elmley Clo. *Kidd* —1B **10**
*Elmley Ho. Redd —4C 24
(off Cardy Clo.)*
Elm Rd. *Kidd* —4G **7**
Elm Rd. *Redd* —4F **25**
Elmstone Clo. *Redd* —5E **29**
Elton Rd. *Bew* —1B **8**
Ely Clo. *Kidd* —4A **6**
Emery Ct. *Kidd* —3E **7**

ndeavour Pl. *Stour S*
—4A 14
nfield. —3F 25
nfield Ind. Est. *Redd* —3F 25
nfield Rd. *Redd* —5F 29
(in two parts)
ngine La. *Stour S* —3H 13
nnerdale Rd. *Stour S* —6H 9
psom Clo. *Redd* —2E 29
psom Rd. *Cats* —1D 18
rica Clo. *Kidd* —1D 6
rneley Clo. *Stour S* —5H 13
rwood Clo. *Redd* —6D 24
ton Wlk. *Hag* —2F 17
ttingley Clo. *Redd* —5B 30
venlode Clo. *Redd* —1H 29
vesham Av. *Redd* —1E 23
(off Burcot La.)
vesham M. *Redd* —5G 25
vesham Rd. *A'wd B* —6G 29
vesham Rd. *Redd* —1F 29
vesham Sq. *Redd* —5G 25
vesham St. *Redd* —5G 25
vesham Wlk. *Redd* —4G 25
wloe Clo. *Redd* —3E 11
xchange St. *Kidd* —5E 7
xeter Clo. *Kidd* —4A 6
xhall Clo. *Redd* —3D 26
xmoor Cres. *Redd* —6D 18
xmoor Dri. *B'gve* —6D 18
yton Clo. *Redd* —5D 26

F
actory La. *B'gve* —3B 22
airbourne Gdns. *Redd*
—2E 29
airfield Ho. *B'gve* —1E 23
(off Burcot La.)
airfield Rd. *B'hth* —1A 18
airford Clo. *Redd* —1E 27
airlight Dri. *B Grn* —1D 20
airmont Rd. *B'gve* —4E 23
airoak Dri. *B'gve* —6B 22
airways Ct. *Kidd* —6G 7
airways Dri. *B'wll* —5B 20
alcon Clo. *Kidd* —1E 11
alconry Cen., The. —5E 17
allowfields Clo. *B'gve*
—1B 22
arfield. *Kidd* —5F 7
arlow Clo. *Redd* —4D 26
arm Clo. *Kidd* —2B 10
armcote Clo. *Redd* —6F 29
armers Rd. *B'gve* —6B 22
ar arm Fld. La. *Redd* —6E 27
ar Moor La. *Redd* —3F 27
arm Rd. *Redd* —5A 26
arm Rd. *Stour S* —1B 14
arnborough Clo. *Redd*
—1F 31
arrier Clo. *B'gve* —6B 22
arthing La. *Redd* —3D 24
eamings Cotts. *Redd* —5F 29
eatherbed La. *H End* —5D 19
eckenham Ho. *B'gve* —1E 23
(off Burcot La.)
eckenham Rd. *H End*
—6D 28
eckenham Rd. *H End &
Head X* —2E 29
elton Clo. *Redd* —1E 31
enwick Clo. *Redd* —1D 28
erguson Dri. *Kidd* —3A 10
erndale Clo. *Cats* —1D 18
erndale Clo. *Hag* —3F 17
erndale Clo. *Stour S* —3C 14
erndale Cres. *Kidd* —2A 6
erndale Housing Est. *Kidd*
—2A 6
erney Hill Av. *Redd* —5B 25
ernleigh. *B'gve* —3D 22
(off New Rd.)
ernwood Rd. *Redd* —5B 30
ield Clo. *Stoke H* —6B 22
ield End. *Stour S* —2G 13
ieldfare Ct. *Kidd* —3G 11
ield La. *Clent* —4H 17
iery Hill Dri. *B Grn* —3D 20
iery Hill Rd. *B Grn* —2C 20

Findon St. *Kidd* —4F 7
Finstall. —3G 23
Finstall Rd. *B'gve & Fins*
—4E 23
Fircroft Clo. *Stoke H* —6A 22
Firecrest Way. *Kidd* —3H 11
Firs Clo. *Kidd* —5G 7
Firs Clo. *Marl* —1F 19
Firs Ind. Est. *Kidd* —5B 10
Firtree Clo. *Redd* —1D 18
Fish Hill. *Redd* —4G 25
Fishing Line Rd. *Redd*
—3G 25
Fladbury Clo. *Redd* —2B 30
Flanders Clo. *Redd* —3D 26
Flats, The. *B'gve* —1C 22
Flavel Rd. *B'gve* —5B 22
Flaxley Clo. *Redd* —4G 27
Flint Clo. *Redd* —2E 11
Flyford Clo. *Redd* —1H 29
Fockbury Mill La. *D'frd &
Redd* —3G 25
Fockbury Rd. *D'frd* —4A 18
Foley Ind. Est. *Kidd* —1C 10
Foley Park. —1B 10
Fordbridge Clo. *Redd* —1E 29
Fordhouse Rd. *B'gve* —3D 22
Ford Rd. *B'gve* —3B 22
Foredraught. *Stud* —6E 31
Foredrift Clo. *Redd* —1G 29
Forelands Gro. *B'gve* —4A 22
Forest Clo. *Bew* —1B 8
Forest Clo. *L End* —4E 19
Forester Way. *Kidd* —1E 11
Forest Vw. *Redd* —4F 29
Forge Dri. *B'gve* —1C 22
Forge La. *Blak* —6A 16
Forge Mill National Needle
Mus. —2H 25
Forge Mill Rd. *Redd* —3H 25
Fort Mahon Pl. *Bew* —1B 8
Foundry St. *Stour S* —2A 14
Four Oaks Clo. *Redd* —2F 29
Fowler Pl. *Stour S* —1A 14
Fownhope Clo. *Redd* —5E 27
Foxcote Clo. *Redd* —4E 27
Foxes Clo. *B'wll* —5C 20
Foxglove Way. *L End* —4F 19
Foxhill Barns. *A'chu* —5F 21
Foxhill La. *A'chu* —4E 21
Foxholes. *Call H* —4B 28
Foxholes, The. *Redd* —2F 7
Foxhollow. *B'gve* —4A 22
Fox La. *B'gve* —4A 22
Foxlydiate. —5A 24
Foxlydiate Clo. *Redd* —5C 24
Foxlydiate Cres. *Redd* —4B 24
Foxlydiate La. *Redd* —5A 24
Foxwalks Av. *B'gve* —4A 22
Franche. —1B 6
Franche Ct. *Kidd* —1B 6
Francecourt Dri. *Kidd* —1B 6
Franche Rd. *Kidd* —2B 6
Franchise St. *Kidd* —5C 6
Francis Rd. *B'gve* —5C 22
Francis Rd. *Stour S* —6A 8
Frankton Clo. *Redd* —2E 31
Freda Eddy Ct. *Kidd* —4E 7
Frederick Rd. *Kidd* —3E 11
Freeman Ct. *Kidd* —1B 10
Fringe Grn. *B'gve* —5D 22
Fringe Grn. Clo. *B'gve*
—5D 22
Fringe Mdw. Rd. *Moons I*
—2F 27
Front Cotts. *A'chu* —4G 21
Fulbrook Clo. *Redd* —3C 26
Fulmar Cres. *Kidd* —2H 11
Fulton Clo. *B'gve* —3E 23
Furrows, The. *Stoke H*
—6A 22
Furze La. *Redd* —4G 27

G
Gainsborough M. *Kidd*
—5B 6
Galahad Way. *Stour S*
—2H 13
Gamson Clo. *Kidd* —6E 7

Ganborough Clo. *Redd*
—1E 31
Gardeners Clo. *Kidd* —2C 6
Gardners Mdw. *Bew* —1D 8
Garganey Ct. *Kidd* —3F 11
Garibaldi Ter. *B'gve* —3D 22
Garland Rd. *Stour S* —6F 9
Garway Clo. *Redd* —1E 31
Gas Sq. *B'gve* —3B 22
Gateley Clo. *Redd* —4G 27
Gaunts, The. *A'chu* —1H 21
Gaydon Clo. *Redd* —1H 29
George Dance Clo. *Kidd*
—4H 7
George Rd. *A'chu* —4H 21
George St. *B'gve* —2C 22
George St. *Kidd* —4F 7
George Wlk. *Redd* —5G 25
Gheluvelt Av. *Kidd* —3F 7
Gheluvelt Ct. *Stour S* —2H 13
Gibb La. *Cats* —2D 18
Gibbons Cres. *Stour S*
—2H 13
Gibbs Rd. *Redd* —3A 26
Gilbert Rd. *B'gve* —5B 22
Gilbert Scott Way. *Kidd* —3F 7
Gilbertstone Clo. *Redd*
—1G 29
Gilgal. *Stour S* —2A 14
Gisburn Clo. *Redd* —3D 24
Glastonbury Clo. *Kidd* —4A 6
Glebe Clo. *Redd* —6D 26
Glebe Rd. *A'chu* —3H 21
Glebe, The. *Beo* —1F 27
Gleneagles Dri. *B'wll* —5B 20
Glenfield Clo. *Redd* —4F 29
Glen, The. *B'wll* —4B 20
Gloucester Way. *Bew* —6D 4
Glover St. *Redd* —5G 25
Godson Cres. *Kidd* —1B 10
Godson Pl. *Kidd* —1C 10
Goldcrest Dri. *Redd* —2H 11
Golden Cross La. *Cats*
—1D 18
Golden Hind Dri. *Stour S*
—4A 14
Goldsmith Wlk. *Kidd* —5H 7
Goldthorne Clo. *Head X*
—1E 29
Goldthorn Pl. *Kidd* —2C 10
Goldthorn Rd. *Kidd* —1B 10
Goodrich Clo. *Redd* —6F 27
Goodwin Clo. *Kidd* —3C 6
Goodwood Rd. *Cats* —1E 19
Goosehill Clo. *Redd* —1E 31
Gorcott Hill. *Beo* —3F 31
Gorsemeadow Dri. *B Grn*
—2C 20
Gould Av. E. *Kidd* —2A 10
Gould Av. W. *Kidd* —3H 9
Grafton Clo. *Redd* —3B 30
Grafton Cres. *B'gve* —5B 22
Grafton Ho. *B'gve* —1E 23
(off Burcot La.)
Grafton La. *U War* —5A 22
Granary Rd. *Stoke H* —6B 22
Granby Clo. *Redd* —4F 27
Grange Ct. *Redd* —4H 25
Grange La. *A'chu* —6F 21
Grange Rd. *Kidd* —3A 6
Grange Rd. *Redd* —3B 6
(nr. Beaufort Av.)
Grange Rd. *Redd* —4H 25
Grangers La. *Redd* —5H 29
Granhill Clo. *Redd* —2A 30
Granville Clo. *B'gve* —3E 23
Granville Crest. *Kidd* —4H 7
Grasmere Clo. *Redd* —3E 7
Grasmere Gro. *Stour S* —6H 9
Gray Clo. *Kidd* —4H 7
Grayshott Clo. *B'gve* —1B 22
Grazing La. *Redd* —6A 24
Gt. Barn La. *Redd* —1D 28
Greatfield Rd. *Kidd* —6B 6
Gt. Western Way. *Stour S*
—1A 14
Greaves Gdns. *Kidd* —1B 6
Greenacres La. *Bew* —6C 4

Greenacres Rd. *B'gve* —1B 22
Greenbank. *B Grn* —2E 21
Greenbank Rd. *Bew* —1A 8
Greendale Clo. *Cats* —2E 19
Greenfield Av. *Marl* —1G 19
Greenfields. *Redd* —6G 25
Greenfinch Clo. *Kidd* —1H 11
Greenford Clo. *Redd* —3D 24
Greenhill. —3G 7
(nr. Kidderminster)
Green Hill. —5A 20
(nr. Linthurst)
Green Hill. *Burc & B'wll*
—6H 19
Greenhill Av. *Kidd* —2F 7
Grn. Hill Clo. *L End* —4G 19
Greenhill Oak. *Kidd* —3F 7
Greenhurst Dri. *B Grn* —1C 20
Greenlands. —2A 30
Greenlands Av. *Redd* —2A 30
Greenlands Bus. Cen. *Redd*
—1B 30
Greenlands Dri. *Redd* —6H 25
Green Lane. —4C 30
Green La. *Call H* —1B 28
Green La. *Cats* —1D 18
Green La. *Stud* —5B 30
Green Mdw. *Stourb* —1G 17
Green Pk. Rd. *B'gve* —3E 23
Grn. Slade Cres. *Marl* —1F 19
Green St. *Kidd* —6E 7
Green St. Ind. Est. *Kidd*
—6E 7
Grn. Sward La. *Redd* —1D 30
Greenway, The. *Hag* —3E 17
Grendon Clo. *Redd* —1D 30
Greystone Clo. *Redd* —2C 26
Griffin Av. *Kidd* —4E 7
Grimley Clo. *Redd* —1H 29
Grimley La. *Fins* —5H 23
Grosvenor Av. *Redd* —4F 7
Grosvenor Gdns. *B'gve*
—5E 19
Grosvenor Wood. *Bew* —1B 8
Grove Gdns. *B'gve* —4D 18
Grove St. *Redd* —4G 25
Grove, The. *Stour S* —4B 14
Guardian Ct. *B'gve* —2D 22
Guild Ct. *B'gve* —2C 22
Guildford Clo. *Kidd* —4A 6
Guild Rd. *B'gve* —3C 22
Guinness Clo. *Redd* —2F 29
Guiting Clo. *Redd* —1D 29
Gunners La. *Stud* —6E 31
Guys Wlk. *B'gve* —5D 18

H
Habberley. —4H 5
Habberley La. *Kidd* —2H 5
Habberley Rd. *Bew & Kidd*
—6F 5
Habberley Rd. *Kidd* —3A 6
Habberley St. *Kidd* —4C 6
Hadzor Ho. *Redd* —4C 24
Hafren Ct. *Bew* —1F 9
Haf ren Way. *Stour S* —2H 13
Hagley. —2H 17
Hagley Clo. *Hag* —2H 17
Hagley Ho. *B'gve* —1E 23
(off Burcot La.)
Hales Park. —1B 8
Hales Pk. *Bew* —1B 8
Halifax Clo. *Kidd* —2A 6
Hall Dri. *Hag* —2H 17
Hall Farm La. *Trim* —2E 5
Hall La. *Hag* —1D 8
Hall Flat. —3F 19
Hamgreen La. *Elc B* —5A 28
Hamilton Clo. *L End* —4F 19
Hamilton Rd. *Kidd* —1B 10
Hamilton Rd. *Redd* —2E 29
Hampton Av. *B'gve* —4D 22
Hampton Clo. *Redd* —3B 30
Hanbury Clo. *B'gve* —5D 18
Hanbury Ho. *Redd* —4D 24
(off Cardy Clo.)
Hanbury Rd. *Stoke H* —6A 22
Hanover Ct. *Redd* —2F 29

Hanover Pl. *B'gve* —3C 22
Hanover St. *B'gve* —2C 22
Hanstone Rd. *Stour S*
—5H 13
Harberrow Clo. *Hag* —2F 17
Harbours Clo. *B'gve* —5A 22
Harbury Clo. *Redd* —1D 30
Hardwick La. *Stud* —5G 31
Hardy Av. *Kidd* —4G 7
Haresfield Clo. *Redd* —6F 25
Hargreaves Ct. *Redd* —1B 10
Harlech Way. *Kidd* —2E 11
Harold Evers Way. *Kidd*
—3F 7
Harport Rd. *Redd* —1A 30
Harriers Grn. *Kidd* —2H 7
Harriers Ind. Est. *Agg* —5F 7
Harrison Rd. *Redd* —2E 29
Harrow Clo. *Hag* —2F 17
Harrow Clo. *Stoke H* —6B 22
Harry Taylor Ho. *Redd*
—5A 26
Hartford Rd. *B'gve* —4E 23
Hartlebury. —4G 15
Hartlebury Castle. —3F 15
Hartlebury Clo. *Redd* —1D 26
Hartlebury Common Nature
Reserve. —4C 14
Hartlebury Rd. *Stour S*
—3B 14
Harvest Clo. *Stoke H* —6A 22
Harvington Clo. *Kidd* —2A 6
Harvington Clo. *Redd* —3D 24
Harvington Rd. *B'gve* —4D 22
Haseley Clo. *Redd* —1E 31
Hastings Rd. *B'gve* —5B 22
Hatfield Clo. *Redd* —1E 31
Haven, The. *B Grn* —2B 20
Hawfinch Ri. *Kidd* —2G 11
Hawford Av. *Kidd* —5G 7
Hawkesbury Clo. *Redd* —3D 26
Hawkstone Clo. *Redd* —2D 6
Hawthorn Coppice. *Hag*
—2F 17
Hawthorn Cres. *Bew* —2A 8
Hawthorn Gro. *Kidd* —4A 6
Hawthorn Rd. *B'gve* —5D 18
Hawthorn Rd. *Redd* —4C 24
Hawthorns, The. *Hag* —4E 17
(off Cavendish Clo.)
Hawthorns, The. *Redd* —4C 24
Haybridge Av. *Hag* —3E 17
Hay Clo. *Kidd* —3C 6
Haydock Rd. *Cats* —1E 19
Haye La. *Map G* —1G 31
Hayford Clo. *Redd* —3A 26
Hayloft Clo. *Stoke H* —6B 22
Haynes Clo. *Cats* —2E 19
Hazeldene. *Stour S* —3C 14
Hazel Rd. *Redd* —3E 25
Hazels, The. *Hag* —3E 17
(off Greenway, The)
Hazelton Clo. *Marl* —2F 19
Hazelton Rd. *Marl* —2F 19
Hazelwood Clo. *Kidd* —6A 6
Headless Cross. —2E 29
Headless Cross Dri. *Redd*
—1F 29
Heath Clo. *Stoke H* —6B 22
Heath Dri. *Kidd* —1H 7
Heathfield Cres. *Kidd* —6B 6
Heathfield Rd. *Bew* —6E 5
Heathfield Rd. *Redd* —1B 28
Heathfield Rd. *Stour S*
—5B 14
Heathlands, The. *Stour S*
—3B 14
Heath La. *Shens* —5H 11
Heath, The. —5G 5
Hedera Rd. *Redd* —2F 27
Hedges Way. *B'gve* —3E 23
Heightington Pl. *Stour S*
—5G 13
Heightington Rd. *Ribb*
—3A 12
Heming Rd. *Redd* —3E 31
Hemmings Entry. *Redd*
—4F 25
Hemming St. *Kidd* —6C 6

Hendy Vs.—Lichfield Av.

Hendy Vs. *Redd* —3C **26**
Henley Rd. *Map G* —6H **27**
Hennals Av. *Redd* —6B **24**
Henry Wlk. *B'gve* —5B **22**
Hentland Clo. *Redd* —4D **26**
Herbert Austin Dri. *Marl*
—1H **19**
Herbert St. *Redd* —4G **25**
Hereford & Worcester
  County Mus. —3F **15**
Hereford Clo. *Kidd* —5A **6**
Hermitage Way. *Stour S*
—5G **13**
Herne's Nest. *Bew* —2C **8**
Heron Clo. *A'chu* —3H **21**
Heronfield Clo. *Redd* —2C **26**
Heronswood Rd. *Kidd* —2F **11**
Hewell Av. *B'gve* —5C **22**
Hewell La. *B Grn* —2D **20**
Hewell La. *Redd* —3A **24**
Hewell Rd. *B Grn* —2E **21**
Hewell Rd. *Redd* —3E **25**
Heydon Rd. *Fins* —3G **23**
Highclere. *Bew* —2C **8**
Highclere Dri. *Bew* —2C **8**
Highfield Av. *Redd* —2F **29**
Highfield Rd. *B'gve* —4B **22**
Highfield Rd. *Kidd* —2G **7**
Highfield Rd. *Redd* —2F **29**
Highfield Rd. *Stud* —6D **30**
Highfields. *B'gve* —3B **22**
Highgate Clo. *Kidd* —6A **6**
Highgrove Ct. *Kidd* —1G **7**
High Habberley. —3H 5
Highlands Clo. *Kidd* —5A **6**
Highland Way. *Redd* —2A **30**
Highley Clo. *Kidd* —2B **10**
Highley Clo. *Redd* —4E **27**
Highlow Av. *Kidd* —1C **6**
High Meadows. *Stoke H*
—6A **22**
High St. *B'gve* —2C **22**
High St. *Bew* —1D **8**
High St. *Kidd* —4E **7**
High St. *Stour S* —3A **14**
High St. *Stud* —6E **31**
High Trees Clo. *Redd* —3G **29**
Hillary Rd. *Stour S* —5D **10**
Hillditch La. *Hartl* —4E **15**
Hill Gro. Cres. *Kidd* —5G **7**
Hillgrove Gdns. *Kidd* —6G **7**
Hill La. *B'gve* —3C **22**
Hill Ri. Vw. *L End* —4F **19**
Hillside. *Redd* —6F **25**
Hillside Clo. *Stour S* —6G **13**
Hillside Dri. *Redd* —3A **6**
Hillside Dri. *L End* —4E **19**
Hill St. *Kidd* —4D **6**
Hill Top. —3A 22
Hill Top. *Redd* —1B **28**
Hilltop Av. *Bew* —6F **5**
Hillview Clo. *L End* —4F **19**
Hillview Rd. *L End* —4F **19**
Himbleton Clo. *Redd* —1H **29**
Hindlip Clo. *Redd* —4E **27**
Hinton Av. *A'chu* —4H **21**
Hinton Fields. *B'hth* —3B **18**
Hither Grn. La. *Redd* —1H **25**
Hoarstone. *Hag* —3E **17**
Hoarstone Clo. *Bew* —5E **5**
Hoarstone La. *Bew* —3E **5**
Hollies, The. *Stour S* —6G **9**
Holloway Dri. *Redd* —6H **25**
Holloway La. *Redd* —5H **25**
Holloway Pk. *Redd* —5A **26**
Hollow Fields Clo. *Redd*
—1G **29**
Hollyberry Clo. *Redd* —4G **27**
Hollyfield Dri. *B Grn* —1B **20**
Holly Gro. *B'gve* —6C **18**
Holly Rd. *Stour S* —2B **14**
Holman St. *Kidd* —5C **6**
Holmcroft Rd. *Kidd* —4G **7**
Holmwood Av. *Kidd* —4A **6**
Holmwood Dri. *Redd* —5E **25**
Holmwood Ho. *Redd* —5E **25**
Holt Hill. *Beo* —1F **27**

Home Mdw. La. *Redd* —1E **27**
Homfray Rd. *Kidd* —1F **7**
Honeybrook. *Kidd* —1B **6**
Honeybrook Gdns. *Kidd*
—1B **6**
Honeybrook La. *Kidd* —1B **6**
Honeysuckle Cotts. *A'chu*
—4G **21**
Hoobrook. —3E 11
Hoobrook Enterprise Cen.
  Kidd —2E **11**
Hoobrook Ind. Est. *Kidd*
—2D **10**
Hoo Farm Ind. Est. *Kidd*
—3E **11**
Hoo Rd. *Kidd* —6E **7**
Hopgardens Av. *B'gve* —2E **23**
Hop Pole La. *Bew* —1A **8**
Hopton Dri. *Kidd* —3E **11**
Hopyard La. *Redd* —5D **26**
Hornbeam Clo. *Bew* —1A **8**
Horngrove. —4H 11
Horse Fair. *Kidd* —3E **7**
Housman Clo. *B'gve* —4B **22**
Housman Ct. *B'gve* —2D **22**
  (off Housman Pk.)
Housman Pk. *B'gve* —2D **22**
Housman Wlk. *Kidd* —4H **7**
Howard Av. *B'gve* —1B **22**
Howard Rd. *Park I* —2B **30**
Huband Clo. *Redd* —3A **26**
Huins Clo. *Redd* —4A **26**
Hume St. *Kidd* —5C **6**
Humphrey Av. *B'gve* —5B **22**
Humphries Dri. *Kidd* —2F **11**
Hunt End. —5E 29
Hunt End La. *Redd* —5E **29**
Huntington Clo. *Redd* —6E **27**
Hurcott. —2H 7
Hurcott Ct. *Kidd* —3F **7**
Hurcott La. *Kidd* —2H **7**
Hurcott Rd. *Kidd* —3E **7**
Hurcott Village. *Kidd* —2H **7**
Husum Way. *Kidd* —3H **7**
Hyde Clo. *B'gve* —2F **23**

Ibis Clo. *Kidd* —1H **11**
Ibstock Clo. *Redd* —4E **27**
Ibstock Ho. *Redd* —4E **27**
Icknield St. *Beo & Chu H*
—1C **26**
Icknield St. *Ips* —6D **26**
Icknield St. Dri. *Redd & Stud*
—6D **26**
Ideal Bldgs. *Kidd* —4D **6**
Illshaw Clo. *Redd* —4G **27**
Ilmington Clo. *Redd* —1D **30**
Imber Rd. *Kidd* —3G **11**
Imperial Av. *Kidd* —2F **7**
Imperial Gro. *Kidd* —2F **7**
Impney Clo. *Redd* —2D **26**
Ingeva Dri. *B Grn* —1B **20**
Ingram Cres. *Bew* —6C **4**
Inn La. *Hartl* —4G **15**
Insetton Clo. *Redd* —4D **26**
Ipsley. —6C 26
Ipsley Alders Nature
  Reserve. —4F **27**
Ipsley Chu. La. *Redd* —6C **26**
Ipsley La. *Redd* —6D **26**
Ipsley St. *Redd* —5G **25**
Ironside Clo. *Bew* —1B **8**
Island Dri. *Kidd* —6E **7**
Ismere Way. *Kidd* —1F **7**
Iverley. —1C 16
Iverley La. *Stourb* —4B **16**
Ivor Rd. *Redd* —6F **25**

Jackson Cres. *Stour S*
—5G **13**
Jacob's Ladder. *Low H* —1F **5**
Jakemans Clo. *Redd* —4E **27**
James Rd. *Kidd* —2G **7**
Jasmine Gro. *B'gve* —6C **18**
Jay Pk. Cres. *Kidd* —2G **11**
Jays Clo. *Redd* —5G **27**
Jelleyman Clo. *Redd* —4B **6**

Jennings Wood La. *H'ton*
—3B **12**
Jersey Clo. *Redd* —1D **26**
Jerusalem Wlk. *Kidd* —3E **7**
Jill La. *Stud* —6B **30**
John's Clo. *Stud* —6C **30**
Johnson Clo. *Redd* —3A **26**
Jordans Clo. *Redd* —4F **29**
Jorden's Wlk. *Bew* —6E **5**
Josiah Mason Mall. *Kidd*
—4E **7**
Jubilee Av. *Redd* —3F **29**
Jubilee Dri. N. *Redd* —2B **10**
Jubilee Dri. S. *Kidd* —2B **10**
Julian Clo. *Cats* —2D **18**
Junction Rd. *B'gve* —1B **22**
Juniper Ct. *Kidd* —6G **7**

Kateshill Ho. *Bew* —2D **8**
Kathleen Fld. Ct. *B'gve*
—1C **22**
Katrine Rd. *Stour S* —5G **9**
Keats Ho. *Redd* —2E **29**
Keats Pl. *Kidd* —4H **7**
Keele Clo. *Redd* —2D **26**
Keith Winter Clo. *B'gve*
—4C **18**
Kelvin Clo. *Kidd* —2A **6**
Kemerton Ho. *Redd* —4C **24**
Kempsey Clo. *Redd* —3B **30**
Kempsford Clo. *Redd* —4H **29**
Kempton Ct. *Cats* —1D **18**
Kenchester Clo. *Redd* —6E **27**
Kendal Clo. *B'gve* —3E **23**
Kendal Clo. *Redd* —5G **27**
Kendal Dri. *Redn* —1E **21**
Kendal End Rd. *Redn* —1E **21**
Kendlewood Rd. *Kidd* —1H **7**
Kenilworth Clo. *Redd* —4F **29**
Kenilworth Dri. *Kidd* —2E **11**
Kennedy Clo. *Kidd* —1F **11**
Kent Clo. *Kidd* —1E **11**
Kenyon Clo. *B'gve* —3D **22**
Kerry Hill. *B'gve* —6B **22**
Kerswell Clo. *Redd* —3D **24**
Kestrel Clo. *Kidd* —1E **11**
Kidderminster. —4E 7
Kidderminster Railway Mus.
—5F **7**
Kidderminster Rd. *Bew*
—1D **8**
Kidderminster Rd. *B'gve*
—1A **22**
Kidderminster Rd. *Hag*
—3F **17**
Kidderminster Rd. *I'ley*
—2A **16**
Kidderminster Rd. S. *Hag*
—5D **16**
Kidderminster Tourist
  Info. Cen. —5F **7**
Kiln Clo. *Stud* —6C **30**
Kilpeck Clo. *Redd* —6F **27**
Kimberley Clo. *Redd* —1B **26**
Kimbolton Dri. *B'will* —5B **20**
Kineton Clo. *Redd* —1D **30**
King Charles Clo. *Kidd* —4C **6**
King Charles Sq. *Kidd* —4E **7**
King Edward Av. *B'gve*
—6C **18**
King Edward Rd. *B'gve*
—5C **18**
Kingfisher Bus. Pk. *Redd*
—5A **26**
Kingfisher Ct. *A'chu* —3A **21**
Kingfisher Gro. *Kidd* —1H **11**
Kingfisher Shop. Cen. *Redd*
—4G **25**
Kingfisher Wlk. *Redd* —4F **25**
King George Av. *B'gve*
—6C **18**
King George Clo. *B'gve*
—6B **18**
Kingham Clo. *Redd* —4F **27**
Kings Arms La. *Stour S*
—6G **13**
Kingscote Clo. *Redd* —1D **26**
Kingsley Av. *Redd* —5A **26**

King's Rd. *Kidd* —4C **6**
Kingsway. *Stour S* —5G **9**
Kinlet Clo. *Redd* —4E **27**
Kinnersley Clo. *Redd* —5E **27**
Kinver Av. *Kidd* —4H **9**
Kinver Dri. *Hag* —1H **17**
Kipling Wlk. *Kidd* —4H **7**
Kitebrook Clo. *Redd* —4E **27**
Kite La. *Redd* —3C **24**
Kittiwake Dri. *Kidd* —1H **11**
Knightsford Clo. *Redd*
—6B **24**
Knottesford Clo. *Stud* —6C **30**
Knowesley Clo. *B'gve* —2E **23**
Knowle Clo. *Redd* —2C **26**
Kylemilne Way. *Stour S*
—3C **14**

Laburnum Clo. *Redd*
—6G **25**
Laburnum Gro. *B'gve* —6C **18**
Laburnum Gro. *Kidd* —2B **6**
Ladbrooke Clo. *Redd* —3G **29**
Ladygrove Clo. *Redd* —2A **30**
Lady Harriet's La. *Redd*
—4H **25**
Lake's Clo. *Kidd* —3C **6**
Lakes Ct. *Bew* —1B **8**
Lakeside. —6A 26
Lakeside. *Redd* —1A **24**
Lakeside Ind. Est. *Redd*
—5A **26**
Lakes Rd., The. *Bew* —1B **8**
Lakes, The. —6B 4
Lambourne Dri. *Bew* —6B **4**
Lancaster Rd. *Bew* —1B **8**
Lancelot Ho. *Kidd* —2H **7**
Land Oak Dri. *Kidd* —2H **7**
Landor Rd. *Redd* —1A **30**
Lane End Wlk. *Stour S*
—6H **13**
Langdale Rd. *Stour S* —5F **13**
Langley Clo. *Redd* —1D **30**
Lansdown Grn. *Redd* —5B **6**
Lapwing Clo. *Kidd* —3H **11**
Lapworth Clo. *Redd* —3H **29**
Larches Cottage Gdns. *Kidd*
—1C **10**
Larches Rd. *Kidd* —1D **10**
Larchmere Dri. *B'gve* —5B **22**
Larford Wlk. *Stour S* —5H **13**
Larkfield Rd. *Redd* —1A **30**
Larkhill. —2E 7
Larkhill. *Kidd* —3E **7**
Lassington Clo. *Redd* —4E **27**
Latchford Clo. *Redd* —2E **27**
Latimer Rd. *A'chu* —5H **21**
Laurel Bank M. *B'will* —6H **21**
Laurel Clo. *Redd* —6G **25**
Laurel Gro. *B'gve* —6C **18**
Lax Lane. *Bew* —1D **8**
Laxton Dri. *Bew* —1B **8**
Layamon Wlk. *Stour S*
—5G **13**
Lea Bank Av. *Kidd* —5A **6**
Lea Castle Clo. *Kidd* —1F **7**
Lea Causeway, The. *Kidd*
—5A **6**
Lea Cft. Rd. *Redd* —5F **29**
Leadbetter Dri. *B'gve* —2A **22**
Lea Pk. Ri. *B'gve* —5C **18**
Leapgate La. *Stour S & Hartl*
—1D **14**
Lea St. *Kidd* —5F **7**
Lea, The. *Kidd* —5A **6**
Leawood Gro. *Kidd* —5A **6**
Lechlade Clo. *Redd* —1B **26**
  (in two parts)
Ledbury Clo. *Redd* —6F **27**
Ledbury Ho. *Redd* —4D **24**
Lench Clo. *Redd* —3C **24**
Lenchville. *Kidd* —1G **7**
Leonard Av. *Kidd* —1G **7**
Leswell Gro. *Kidd* —4F **7**
Leswell La. *Kidd* —4F **7**
Leswell St. *Kidd* —4F **7**
Leysters Clo. *Redd* —5E **27**
Lichfield Av. *Kidd* —4H **5**

Lichfield St. *Stour S* —3A **14**
Lickey End. —4F 19
Lickey Grange Dri. *Marl*
—1H **19**
Lickey Gro. *Kidd* —2B **10**
Lickey Rock. —2G 19
Lickey Rock. *Marl* —1G **19**
Lickhill. —1F 13
Lickhill Rd. *Stour S* —2H **13**
Lickhill Rd. N. *Stour S* —6F **9**
Lightoak Clo. *Redd* —4E **29**
Lilac Clo. *Redd* —6G **25**
Lilac Gro. *Stour S* —2G **13**
Lilleshall Clo. *Redd* —5E **27**
Lily Grn. La. *Redd* —3C **24**
Lime Ct. *Kidd* —6G **7**
Lime Gro. *B'gve* —6C **18**
Lime Tree Cres. *Redd* —4D **24**
Lime Tree Wlk. *Stour S*
—1G **13**
Lincoln Cres. *Kidd* —4H **5**
Lincoln Rd. *B'gve* —6B **18**
Lincomb La. *Stour S* —6D **14**
Linden Av. *Kidd* —3G **7**
Linden Av. *Stour S* —5G **13**
Linden Gdns. *Kidd* —4G **7**
Linden Gro. *Kidd* —3G **7**
Lindridge Clo. *Redd* —5G **27**
Lineholt Clo. *Redd* —4A **30**
Linehouse La. *Marl & L End*
—1G **19**
Lingen Clo. *Redd* —5E **27**
Lingfield Rd. *Bew* —5F **5**
Lingfield Wlk. *Cats* —1E **19**
Links, The. *Kidd* —6G **7**
Linnet Ri. *Kidd* —3F **11**
Linthurst. —4B 20
Linthurst Newtown. *B'will*
—4B **20**
Linthurst Rd. *B'will & B Grn*
—4B **20**
Linton Clo. *Redd* —6F **27**
Linton M. *Redd* —6F **27**
  (in two parts)
Lion Hill. *Stour S* —3A **14**
Lion Sq. *Kidd* —4E **7**
Lion St. *Kidd* —4E **7**
Lisle Av. *Kidd* —1C **10**
Lister Rd. *Kidd* —1B **10**
Lit. Acre. *Redd* —4F **29**
Lit. Forge Rd. *Redd* —2C **30**
Lit. Grebe Rd. *Kidd* —1H **11**
Little Heath. —4G 19
Littleheath La. *L End* —4F **19**
Little La. *B'gve* —2C **22**
Littlewoods. *Redd* —5F **29**
Llangorse Clo. *Stour S* —5G **9**
Load St. *Bew* —1D **8**
Lobelia Clo. *Kidd* —1C **6**
Lock Clo. *Redd* —4C **24**
Lodge Clo. *Bew* —4F **5**
Lodge Cres. *Hag* —3G **17**
Lodge Park. —6H 25
Lodge Pool Dri. *Redd* —1H **29**
Lodge Rd. *Redd* —5G **25**
Lodge Rd. *Stour S* —3A **14**
Lombard St. *Stour S* —2A **14**
Long Acre. *Kidd* —3F **7**
Longboat La. *Stour S* —2A **14**
Longborough Clo. *Redd*
—4D **28**
Long Clo. *Hag* —4E **17**
Long Compton Dri. *Hag*
—2F **17**
Longdon Clo. *Redd* —3B **30**
Long Eye. —5G 19
Longfellow Clo. *Redd* —3E **29**
Longfellow Grn. *Kidd* —4H **7**
Longhope Clo. *Redd* —4G **27**
Longlands, The. *B Grn*
—3E **21**
Long Mdw. Rd. *L End* —4F **19**
Longmoor Clo. *Redd* —2D **24**
Longmynd Way. *Stour S*
—5F **13**
Lord Austin Dri. *Marl* —1H **19**
Lordswood Clo. *Redd* —6B **24**
Lorne Gro. *Kidd* —4G **7**
Lorne St. *Kidd* —5G **7**

Lorne St. *Stour S* —1A **14**
Lovage Rd. *Redd* —2F **27**
Love Lyne. *H End* —4B **28**
Lowans Hill Vw. *Redd*
—4E **25**
Lowe La. *Kidd* —1B **6**
Lower Clent. —4H 17
Lwr. Common La. *Redd*
—6D **24**
Lwr. Gambolds La. *Fins*
—6E **23**
Lwr. Grinsty La. *Call H*
—3C **28**
Lower Heath. —5B 14
Lwr. Lickhill Rd. *Stour S*
—1F **13**
Lower Marlbrook. —1F 19
Lwr. Mill St. *Kidd* —4D **6**
Lower Pk. *Bew* —1D **8**
Lwr. Parklands. *Kidd* —5C **6**
Lwr. Shepley La. *L End*
—4G **19**
Lowes Hill. —5D 18
Loweswater Rd. *Stour S*
—5G **9**
Lowfield La. *Redd* —3D **24**
Low Habberley. —2H 5
Low Hill. —5G 11
Lowlands La. *Redd* —5D **26**
Loxley Clo. *Redd* —2D **26**
Lucy Edwards Ct. *Kidd* —5C **6**
Ludgate Av. *Redd* —5A **6**
Ludlow Rd. *Kidd* —2E **11**
Ludlow Rd. *Redd* —5F **25**
Lupton Ct. *B'gve* —3D **22**
Lydham Clo. *Redd* —3G **25**
Lydney Clo. *Redd* —1D **26**
Lygon Clo. *Redd* —3A **26**
Lynden Clo. *B'gve* —1B **22**
Lyndenwood. *Redd* —6C **24**
Lyndholm Rd. *Kidd* —4G **7**
Lyndhurst Dri. *Redd* —2E **7**
Lynwood Dri. *Blak* —6A **16**
Lyttelton Av. *B'gve* —5B **22**
Lyttelton Pl. *Hag* —2H **17**
Lyttelton Rd. *Bew* —6C **4**

Mabey Av. *Redd* —3H **25**
Madeley Rd. *Moons I* —3F **27**
Magpie Way. *Kidd* —2H **11**
Mainstone Clo. *Redd* —5E **27**
Maisemore Clo. *Redd* —1D **26**
Malcolm Av. *B'gve* —1B **22**
Malfield Dri. *Redd* —5B **24**
Malham Rd. *Stour S* —5G **9**
Mallard Av. *Kidd* —1H **11**
Mallard Clo. *Redd* —3H **25**
Mallard Rd. *Stud* —6F **31**
Mallory Dri. *Kidd* —1D **6**
Maltings, The. *Stud* —6D **30**
Malvern Clo. *Stour S* —6F **13**
Malvern Dri. *Kidd* —1E **11**
Malvern Ho. *Redd* —1E **29**
Malvern Rd. *B'gve* —5A **22**
Malvern Rd. *Redd* —2F **29**
Malvern Vw. *Kidd* —3B **10**
Mandarin Av. *Kidd* —1H **11**
Mandeville Way. *B'gve*
—5D **18**
Manor Av. *Kidd* —3A **6**
Manor Av. S. *Kidd* —3A **6**
Manor Clo. *Kidd* —4A **6**
Manor Clo. *Stour S* —1B **14**
Manor Ct. Rd. *B'gve* —4B **22**
Manor M. *Stud* —6E **31**
Manor Rd. *Stour S* —1A **14**
Manor Rd. *Stud* —6E **31**
Mansell Rd. *Redd* —3F **29**
Maple Clo. *B'gve* —2B **6**
Maple Clo. *Stour S* —2G **13**
Mappleborough Clo. *Redd*
—3D **24**
Mappleborough Green.
—2G 31
Marble All. *Stud* —6E **31**
March Gro. *Bew* —6D **4**
Marchwood Clo. *Redd*
—3C **24**

Margesson Dri. *B Grn* —1E **21**
Market Pl. *Kidd* —2C **22**
Market Pl. *Redd* —4G **25**
Market St. *B'gve* —2C **22**
Market St. *Kidd* —5E **7**
Market Wlk. *Redd* —4G **25**
Market Way. *Hag* —2H **17**
Marlborough Av. *B'gve*
—5D **22**
Marlborough Ct. *B'gve*
—4E **23**
Marlborough Dri. *Stour S*
—6G **13**
Marlborough St. *Kidd* —5E **7**
Marlbrook La. *Marl* —6G **19**
Marlfield Rd. *B'gve* —5E **23**
Marlfield. *Redd* —3B **26**
Marlfield La. *Redd* —4B **26**
(in two parts)
Marlowe Clo. *Kidd* —4H **7**
Marlpit La. *Redd* —1D **28**
(in two parts)
Marlpool Clo. *Kidd* —1B **6**
Marlpool Dri. *Redd* —5E **25**
Marlpool La. *Kidd* —1C **6**
Marlpool Pl. *Kidd* —2B **6**
Marsden Rd. *Redd* —5G **25**
Marshfield Clo. *Redd* —1B **26**
Marsh Way. *Cats* —1C **18**
Martin Clo. *B'gve* —3B **22**
Martingale Clo. *B'gve* —6B **22**
Martins Way. *Stour S* —3H **13**
Mart La. *Stour S* —3A **14**
Martley Clo. *Redd* —3B **30**
Martley Rd. *Stour S* —6F **13**
Masefield Gdns. *Redd* —4H **7**
Mason Clo. *Redd* —3F **29**
Mason Rd. *Kidd* —4C **6**
Mason Rd. *Redd* —3E **29**
Matchborough. —1E 31
Matchborough Shop. Cen.
Redd —1E **31**
Matchborough Way. *Redd*
—3E **31**
Matthew La. *Stour S* —2G **13**
Maund Clo. *B'gve* —5B **22**
Maxstoke Clo. *Redd* —1D **30**
Mayberry Clo. *Stour S*
—2G **13**
Mayfield Clo. *Cats* —1C **18**
Mayfield Clo. *Kidd* —2A **6**
Mayfields. *Redd* —6F **25**
Mayfields, The. *Redd* —6F **25**
Mayflower Clo. *Stour S*
—4A **14**
Maypole Clo. *Bew* —1E **9**
McConnell Clo. *B'gve* —5E **23**
Meadow Cft. *Hag* —4E **17**
Meadow Hill Clo. *Kidd* —5A **6**
Meadowhill Cres. *Redd*
—3H **25**
Meadowhill Rd. *Redd* —3H **25**
Meadow La. *A'chu* —1H **21**
Meadow Mills Est. *Kidd*
—5E **7**
Meadow Ri. *Bew* —6E **5**
Meadows, The. *Stourb*
—1G **17**
Meadowvale Rd. *L End*
—4F **19**
Meadow Vw. *Stour S* —6G **13**
Meadway, The. *Redd* —1E **29**
Mearse La. *B Grn* —2A **20**
Medici Rd. *B'gve* —2F **23**
Meir Rd. *Redd* —2C **30**
Melbourne Av. *B'gve* —6B **18**
Melbourne Clo. *B'gve* —1B **22**
Melbourne Rd. *B'gve* —6B **18**
Melen St. *Redd* —4F **25**
Mendip Clo. *B'gve* —5D **18**
Mendip Ho. *Redd* —2D **26**
Menteith Clo. *Stour S* —5G **9**
Mercia Clo. *B'gve* —5C **22**
Mercot Clo. *Redd* —4A **30**
Meredith Grn. *Kidd* —3A **10**
Merevale Clo. *Redd* —2D **30**
Merganser Way. *Kidd* —2H **11**
Meriden Clo. *Redd* —5G **27**
Meridian Pl. *B'gve* —3D **22**

Merlin Dri. *Kidd* —1H **11**
Merricks Clo. *Bew* —1B **8**
Merricks La. *Bew* —1B **8**
Merriemont Dri. *B Grn*
—1B **20**
Merrill Gdns. *Marl* —1G **19**
Merse Rd. *Moons I & Redd*
—2E **27**
Merton Clo. *Bew* —6B **4**
Merton Clo. *Redd* —3G **7**
Michaelwood Clo. *Redd*
—6B **24**
Mickleton Clo. *Redd* —3G **29**
Middlefield La. *Hag* —2G **17**
Middlefield Rd. *B'gve* —5E **23**
Middle Ho. Dri. *Marl* —1G **19**
Middlehouse La. *Redd*
—2G **25**
Middlemore Clo. *Stud*
—6D **30**
Middle Piece Dri. *Redd*
—6C **24**
Middleton Clo. *Redd* —6F **27**
Middleton M. *Redd* —6F **27**
Middleton Rd. *B'gve* —6C **18**
Middleton Rd. *Redd* —1C **6**
Milcote Clo. *Redd* —3H **25**
Milestone Dri. *Hag* —4E **17**
Milford Av. *Stour S* —6G **9**
Milford Clo. *Redd* —3D **28**
Milhill Rd. *Redd* —1E **31**
Mill Clo. *Blak* —6A **16**
Mill Clo. *B'gve* —6C **22**
Mill Clo. *Stour S* —3B **14**
Milldale Clo. *Redd* —2E **7**
Millfield Gdns. *Kidd* —4D **6**
Millfield Rd. *B'gve* —3A **22**
Mill La. *Blak* —6A **16**
Mill La. *B'gve* —2C **22**
Mill La. *Kidd* —2F **11**
(DY10)
Mill La. *Kidd* —4D **6**
(nr. Mill St.)
Mill La. *Stour S* —2B **14**
Millpool Clo. *Hag* —4F **17**
Millrace Rd. *Redd* —2G **25**
Millridge Way. *Ware* —5F **15**
Mill Rd. *Stour S* —2B **14**
Millsborough Rd. *Redd*
(in two parts) —5G **25**
Millside Ct. *Bew* —1D **8**
Mill St. *Kidd* —3C **6**
Mill St. *Redd* —4F **25**
Milton Clo. *Kidd* —4A **6**
Milton Clo. *Redd* —2E **29**
Milton Dri. *Hag* —1H **17**
Milton Rd. *Cats* —2D **18**
Milward Sq. *Redd* —5G **25**
Minster Clo. *Stour S* —2A **14**
Minster Wlk. *Cats* —2C **18**
Minton M. *B'gve* —4E **23**
Minworth Clo. *Redd* —6D **24**
Mitcheldean Clo. *Redd*
—3G **29**
Mitre Ct. *B'gve* —1D **22**
(off Strand, The)
Mitton Clo. *Stour S* —2A **14**
Mitton Gdns. *Stour S* —3A **14**
Mitton St. *Stour S* —3A **14**
Mitton Wlk. *Stour S* —3A **14**
Moat Mill La. *B'gve* —3B **22**
Moffit Way. *Stour S* —2G **13**
Monarch's Way. *Hag* —2G **17**
Monarch's Way. *Stourb*
—3D **16**
Monks Dri. *Stud* —6D **30**
Monks Path. *Redd* —1B **26**
Montgomery Clo. *Cats*
—1D **18**
Monument La. *Hag* —1H **17**
Moons Moat. —3F 27
Moons Moat Dri. *Redd*
—3D **26**
Moorcroft Clo. *Call H* —4D **28**
Moorcroft Gdns. *Call H*
—4D **28**
Moorfield Dri. *B'gve* —1C **22**
Moorgate Clo. *Redd* —2E **27**

Moor Hall Dri. *Stour S*
—2H **13**
Moorhall La. *Stour S* —2G **13**
Moors Av. *Hartl* —4H **15**
Moorsom Way. *B'gve* —6D **22**
Mordiford Clo. *Redd* —5E **27**
Morella Clo. *Bew* —1B **8**
Morillon Ct. *Kidd* —3G **11**
Morris Wlk. *B'gve* —4B **22**
Morsefield La. *Redd* —1D **30**
Mortimer Gro. *Bew* —6D **4**
Morton Ho. *Redd* —5C **24**
Morton La. *Redd* —4D **28**
Moss La. *Beo* —1F **27**
Moss La. *Beo* —1F **27**
Mostyn Rd. *Stour S* —6G **9**
Moule Clo. *Kidd* —4B **6**
Mt. Pleasant. *Redd* —1F **29**
Mount Rd. *Fair* —1A **18**
Mount St. *Redd* —6G **25**
Mt. Vernon Dri. *B'gve*
—5D **18**
Mouse La. *Kidd* —2B **6**
Munro Clo. *Kidd* —4H **7**
Munsley Clo. *Redd* —6F **27**
Musketts Ct. *Redd* —6D **24**
Musketts Way. *Redd* —6E **25**
Muskoka. *Bew* —1B **8**
Myrtle Av. *Redd* —6G **25**

Nailers Clo. *Stoke H* —6B **22**
Nailers Ct. *B'gve* —2C **22**
Nailsworth Rd. *Redd* —6H **25**
Nairn Clo. *Redd* —4E **27**
Napton Clo. *Redd* —1D **30**
Naseby Clo. *Redd* —2D **26**
Nash Clo. *Kidd* —5H **7**
Naylor Clo. *Kidd* —1E **11**
Needle Clo. *Stud* —6E **31**
Needle Mill La. *Redd* —2G **25**
Neighbrook Clo. *Redd*
—6B **24**
Nelson Rd. *Stour S* —6B **14**
Netherfield. *Redd* —2A **30**
Netherton La. *Bew* —2C **8**
Netherton Rd. *Dunl* —6A **12**
Neville Av. *Kidd* —1D **10**
Neville Clo. *Redd* —3H **25**
Neville Ct. *Kidd* —1D **10**
New Bldgs. *Kidd* —4G **6**
Newbury Clo. *Cats* —1E **19**
Newent Clo. *Redd* —5G **27**
Newfield Gdns. *Hag* —4F **17**
Newfield Rd. *Hag* —4F **17**
Newland Clo. *Redd* —3B **30**
Newlands Clo. *Kidd* —3C **6**
New Mdw. Rd. *Redd* —5B **26**
Newport Clo. *Redd* —4D **28**
Newport Ter. *Kidd* —1D **10**
New Rd. *Bew* —5F **5**
New Rd. *B'gve* —2C **22**
New Rd. *Kidd* —6E **7**
New Rd. *Side* —1B **18**
(nr. Stourbridge Rd.)
New Rd. *Side* —1B **18**
(nr. Willow Rd.)
New Rd. *Stud* —6E **31**
New St. *Stour S* —3H **13**
Newton Clo. *Bew* —6B **4**
Newton Clo. *Redd* —4A **30**
Newton Rd. *B'gve* —5D **22**
New Wlk. *Redd* —4G **25**
Nightingale Dri. *Kidd* —2H **11**
Nina Clo. *Stour S* —3B **14**
Nine Days La. *Redd* —4B **30**
Noel Ct. *Redd* —2E **29**
Norbury Clo. *Redd* —1B **26**
Norgrove La. *B'ley* —4A **28**
Northcliffe Heights. *Kidd*
—3C **6**
Northfield Clo. *Redd* —2D **26**
Northgate Clo. *Redd* —4A **6**
Northleach Clo. *Redd* —3B **26**
N. Moons Moat Ind. Area.
Redd —3E **27**
North Rd. *B'gve* —2D **22**
North Rd. *Stour S* —1A **14**
Northside Clo. *Redd* —3G **29**

Northumberland Av. *Kidd*
—1C **10**
Northwood La. *Bew* —3B **4**
Norton Clo. *Redd* —6F **27**
Norton Rd. *Kidd* —4H **7**
Norwich Av. *Kidd* —4H **5**
Nursery Clo. *Hag* —4F **17**
Nursery Clo. *Kidd* —2B **6**
Nursery Gro. *Kidd* —2B **6**
Nursery Rd. *Bew* —6D **4**

Oakalls Av. *B'gve* —2E **23**
Oak Apple Clo. *Stour S*
—6G **13**
Oak Apple Rd. *Cats* —2E **19**
Oakdene. *Stour S* —3B **14**
Oakdene Dri. *B Grn* —2D **20**
Oakenshaw. —4G 29
Oakenshaw Rd. *Redd* —2H **29**
Oakfield Rd. *Kidd* —5B **6**
Oak Gro. *Kidd* —6G **7**
Oakham Clo. *Redd* —5A **30**
Oakhampton Rd. *Stour S*
—6G **13**
Oakhill Av. *Kidd* —6E **7**
Oakhurst Dri. *B'gve* —1D **22**
Oakland Gro. *B'gve* —6E **19**
Oaklands, The. *Kidd* —3G **7**
Oakley Ho. *B'gve* —3D **22**
Oakly Rd. *Redd* —5F **25**
Oakridge Clo. *Redd* —1C **26**
Oak Rd. *Cats* —2E **19**
Oak Tree Av. *Redd* —4D **24**
Oak Tree Clo. *A'chu* —3H **21**
Oakwood Rd. *Bew* —1B **8**
Oasthouse Clo. *Stoke H*
—6A **22**
Offenham Clo. *Redd* —2B **26**
Offmore Farm. —4G 7
Offmore Farm Clo. *Kidd*
—4H **7**
Offmore La. *Kidd* —4G **7**
Offmore Rd. *Kidd* —4F **7**
Offwell Clo. *Redd* —1D **30**
Old Bakery Ct. *Hag* —3F **17**
Old Birmingham Rd. *L End &
Marl* —3F **19**
Oldbury Clo. *Redd* —2B **26**
Old Chester Rd. S. *Kidd*
—2E **11**
Old Crest Av. *Redd* —6G **25**
Oldfields. *Hag* —2G **17**
Old Ford Wlk. *Stour S*
—6G **13**
Old Forge Dri. *Redd* —6B **26**
Old Forge Gdns. *Hartl*
—4H **15**
Oldington La. *Kidd* —4B **10**
Oldington Trad. Est. *Kidd*
—3B **10**
Oldnall Rd. *Kidd* —6F **7**
Old Rectory La. *A'chu* —3H **21**
Old Sta. Rd. *B'gve* —3C **22**
Old Stratford Rd. *B'gve*
—2F **23**
Old Vicarage Gdns. *Stud*
—6E **31**
Olive Gro. *Stour S* —2H **13**
Olympus Gdns. *Stour S*
—3C **14**
Ombersley Clo. *Redd* —3B **30**
Orchard Clo. *Hag* —4G **17**
Orchard Clo. *Stour S* —2B **14**
Orchard Cft. *B Grn* —2E **21**
Orchard Pl. *Map G* —2F **31**
Orchard Ri. *Bew* —1C **8**
Orchard Rd. *B'gve* —6C **18**
Orchards, The. *Redd* —1B **6**
Orchard St. *Kidd* —4E **7**
Orchard St. *Redd* —5G **25**
Oriole Gro. *Kidd* —2H **11**
Osborne Clo. *Kidd* —4H **7**
Osnor Ct. *B'gve* —5E **23**
Osprey Pk. Dri. *Kidd* —1H **11**
Oswald St. *Redd* —5G **25**
Oswestry Clo. *Redd* —1D **26**
Other Rd. *Redd* —4G **25**

Otter Clo.—Sandy Bank

Otter Clo. *Redd* —5F **27**
Oulton Clo. *Kidd* —2D **6**
Ounty John La. *Stourb* —1E **17**
Outwood Clo. *Redd* —3G **29**
Oversley Clo. *Redd* —3C **24**
Oxford St. *Kidd* —4E **7**
Oxhill Clo. *Redd* —1E **31**
Oxleasow Rd. *Redd* —4E **27**

Packwood Clo. *Redd* —1B **28**
Paddock La. *Redd* —3G **29**
Paddock, The. *Stoke H* —6A **22**
Padgets La. *Redd* —4D **26**
Paget Clo. *B'gve* —2B **22**
Painswick Clo. *Redd* —4G **29**
Palmers Rd. *Redd* —3F **27**
Palmyra Rd. *B'gve* —2F **23**
Paper Mill Dri. *Redd* —3B **26**
Papworth Dri. *B'gve* —5C **18**
Parade, The. *Kidd* —2F **7**
Paradise Row. *B'gve* —2C **22**
Parish Hill. *B'hth* —1A **18**
Park Av. *Stour S* —2H **13**
Pk. Butts Ringway. *Kidd* —4D **6**
Park Clo. *Bew* —1C **8**
Park Ct. *Redd* —5A **26**
Park Cres. *Stour S* —2H **13**
Park Dingle. *Bew* —2A **8**
Parkes Pas. *Stour S* —3A **14**
Park Farm. —2B 30
Park Farm Ind. Est. *Park I* —3D **30**
Park Farm Ind. Est. *Redd* —3C **30**
Park Farm South. —4D 30
Parkfield Clo. *Hartl* —4G **15**
Parkfield Clo. *Redd* —2B **26**
Parkland Av. *Kidd* —5B **6**
Parklands Clo. *Redd* —3C **24**
Park La. *Bew* —2B **8**
Park La. *Kidd* —4D **6**
Park La. Ind. Est. *Kidd* —6D **6**
Park Rd. *Hag* —3F **17**
Parkside. *B'gve* —1D **22**
Parkstone Av. *B'gve* —4A **22**
Park St. *Kidd* —4D **6**
Park Wlk. *Redd* —5G **25**
Park Way. *Redd* —3A **26**
Parkwood Rd. *B'gve* —1B **22**
Parmington Clo. *Call H* —4D **28**
Parry Rd. *Kidd* —1B **10**
Parsons La. *Hartl* —6F **15**
Parsons Rd. *Redd* —6G **25**
Partridge Gro. *Kidd* —2G **11**
Partridge La. *Call H* —4C **28**
Patchetts La. *Bew* —6C **4**
Patch La. *Redd* —4H **29**
Pat Davis Ct. *Kidd* —3E **7**
Paternoster Row. *Kidd* —4D **6**
Patios, The. *Kidd* —3C **6**
Pavilion Gdns. *B'gve* —5C **18**
Paxford Clo. *Redd* —2B **26**
Paxton Clo. *B'gve* —3E **23**
Peakman St. *Redd* —4G **25**
Pearl La. *Stour S* —5F **13**
Peart Dri. *Stud* —6C **30**
Pear Tree Clo. *Kidd* —3H **7**
Pebworth Clo. *Redd* —1C **26**
Pedmore Clo. *Redd* —3B **30**
Peel St. *Kidd* —5D **6**
Pelham Lodge. *Kidd* —5F **7**
Pembridge Clo. *Redd* —5D **26**
Pembroke Way. *Stour S* —6G **9**
Penmanor. *Fins* —3G **23**
Pennine Rd. *B'gve* —5D **18**
Pennyford Clo. *Redd* —3C **24**
Penstock Ct. *Kidd* —2H **7**
Penzer Dri. *B Grn* —2E **21**
Peregrine Gro. *Kidd* —2G **11**
Perrett Wlk. *Kidd* —4D **6**
Perrin Av. *Kidd* —6B **6**
Perryfields. —6A 18
Perryfields Clo. *Redd* —5H **29**
Perryfields Cres. *B'gve* —5C **18**
Perryfields Rd. *B'gve* —1A **22**
Perry La. *B'gve* —2C **22**
Perry La. *Tort* —1H **15**
Pershore Rd. *Kidd* —4A **6**
Peterbrook Clo. *Redd* —3H **29**
Peter's Finger. *B'gve* —3C **22**
Petton Clo. *Redd* —5F **27**
Pewterers All. *Bew* —6D **4**
Pheasant Clo. *Kidd* —2G **11**
Pheasant La. *Redd* —4G **29**
Philips Ter. *Redd* —4H **25**
Pike Hill. *B'wll* —3B **20**
(in two parts)
Pikes Pool La. *Fins & Burc* —3G **23**
Pinedene. *Stour S* —3B **14**
Pineridge Dri. *Kidd* —5B **6**
Pine Tree Clo. *Redd* —5B **24**
Pinetree Rd. *Bew* —2B **8**
Pine Wlk. *Stour S* —2G **13**
Pinewood Clo. *Kidd* —1C **6**
Pinewoods Av. *Hag* —4E **17**
Pinewoods Clo. *Hag* —4E **17**
Pinewoods Ct. *Hag* —4E **17**
Pinfield Dri. *B Grn* —1C **20**
Pink Green. —1H 27
Pink Grn. La. *Redd* —4C **24**
Pinta Dri. *Stour S* —3B **14**
Pintail Gro. *Kidd* —1H **11**
Pinvin Ho. *Redd* —4C **24**
Pipers Clo. *B'gve* —5A **22**
Pipers Rd. *Park I* —4D **30**
Pipit Ct. *Kidd* —2G **11**
Pitcheroak Cotts. *Redd* —5C **24**
Pitts La. *Kidd* —4E **7**
Pitt St. *Kidd* —1G **7**
Planetree Clo. *B'gve* —2E **23**
Plane Tree Clo. *Kidd* —3F **7**
Pleasant Harbour. *Bew* —6D **4**
Pleasant St. *Kidd* —3E **7**
Plimsoll St. *Kidd* —5D **6**
Ploughmans Wlk. *Stoke H* —6A **22**
Plover Gro. *Kidd* —3H **11**
Plymouth Clo. *Redd* —6E **25**
Plymouth Ct. *Redd* —1E **29**
Plymouth Dri. *B Grn* —2B **20**
Plymouth Rd. *B Grn* —1B **20**
Plymouth Rd. *Redd* —6F **25**
Plymouth Rd. S. *Redd* —1E **29**
Pochard Clo. *Kidd* —3F **11**
Polesworth Clo. *Redd* —1D **30**
Pool Bank. *Redd* —1F **29**
Pooles Ct. *Kidd* —3E **7**
Pool Pl. *Redd* —5G **25**
Pool Rd. *Stud* —6E **31**
Poplar Clo. *Cats* —2C **18**
Poplar Dri. *B Grn* —2E **21**
Poplar Rd. *Kidd* —6C **6**
Poplar Rd. *Redd* —5C **24**
Poplar Row. *Kidd* —6C **6**
Power Sta. Rd. *Stour S* —4A **14**
Pratts La. *Map G* —3F **31**
Prestbury Clo. *Redd* —5G **27**
Preston Clo. *Redd* —2B **26**
Priestfield Rd. *Redd* —5G **29**
Primrose Clo. *L End* —4F **19**
Prince Rupert Rd. *Stour S* —4G **13**
Princess Way. *Stour S* —5G **13**
Prior Clo. *Kidd* —5H **7**
Priors Oak. *Redd* —4D **24**
Priory Sq. *Stud* —5E **31**
Priory, The. *Stour S* —1A **14**
Pritchard Ct. *Bew* —1D **8**
Proctors Barn La. *Redd* —4B **26**
Prophet's Clo. *Redd* —5F **25**
Prospect Hill. *Kidd* —4E **7**
Prospect Hill. *Redd* —4G **25**
Prospect La. *Kidd* —4E **7**
Prospect Rd. *Stour S* —2A **14**
Prospect Rd. N. *Redd* —4A **26**
Prospect Rd. S. *Redd* —4A **26**
Prospect Ter. *Kidd* —4E **7**
Proud Cross Ringway. *Kidd* —4C **6**
Providence Rd. *B'gve* —1C **22**
Pullman Clo. *Stour S* —2A **14**
Pumphouse La. *B Grn & B'wll* —2A **20**
Pumphouse La. *Redd* —1A **28**
Pump St. *Kidd* —6E **7**
Purcell Ho. *Kidd* —4H **5**
Purshall Clo. *Redd* —5E **25**
Puxton Dri. *Kidd* —1D **6**
Puxton La. *Kidd* —3C **6**

Quail Pk. Dri. *Kidd* —2G **11**
Quantock Dri. *Kidd* —4G **7**
Quarry Bank. *Hartl* —4G **15**
Quarry La. *B'gve* —4A **22**
Quarry, The. *Kidd* —2F **7**
Queen Elizabeth Rd. *Kidd* —4H **7**
Queen's Cotts. *Redd* —4D **24**
Queen's Rd. *Stour S* —5H **13**
Queen St. *Kidd* —3E **7**
Queen St. *Redd* —4G **25**
Queens Way. *Bew* —5E **5**
Quibery Clo. *Redd* —5F **27**
Quinneys La. *Redd* —4B **30**
Quinton Clo. *Redd* —1D **30**

Radford Av. *Kidd* —3E **7**
Radford Ho. *Redd* —4C **24**
Radford Rd. *A'chu* —1H **21**
Radway Clo. *Redd* —2B **26**
Raglan Ct. *B'gve* —3D **22**
Ragley Cres. *B'gve* —4D **22**
Ragley Ho. *Redd* —4C **24**
Raglis Clo. *Redd* —6C **24**
Railway Clo. *Stud* —6D **30**
Randall Av. *A'chu* —4H **21**
Rangeways Rd. *Kidd* —2A **6**
Rangeworthy Clo. *Redd* —3E **29**
Rannoch Clo. *Stour S* —5G **9**
Ravensbank Bus. Pk. *Redd* —2F **27**
Ravensbank Dri. *Moons I & Redd* —1C **26**
Ravensmere Rd. *Redd* —1B **30**
Raven St. *Stour S* —3H **13**
Rear Cotts. *A'chu* —4G **21**
Recreation Rd. *B'gve* —1C **22**
Rectory La. *Hartl* —3G **15**
Rectory La. *Stour S* —4F **13**
Rectory Rd. *Redd* —1F **29**
Redcar Clo. *Cats* —1D **18**
Red Cross. —1A 22
Redditch. —4G 25
Redditch Ringway. *Redd* —4F **25**
Redditch Rd. *A'chu* —2H **21**
Redditch Rd. *Stoke H* —6A **22**
Redditch Rd. *Stud* —5D **30**
Redditch Tourist Info. Cen. —5G 25
Red Hill. *Bew* —2D **8**
Red Hill. *Redd* —6H **25**
Red Hill Gro. *Stud* —4E **31**
Redhouse Rd. *Stour S* —6F **13**
Redlake Dri. *Stourb* —1G **17**
Redland Clo. *Marl* —1F **19**
Red Lion St. *A'chu* —1H **21**
Red Lion St. *Redd* —4G **25**
Red Sands Rd. *Kidd* —2E **7**
Redstart Av. *Kidd* —2H **11**
Redstone Clo. *Redd* —2C **26**
Redstone La. *Stour S* —6G **13**
Redstone Nature Reserve. —5A 14
Redwing Ct. *Kidd* —3G **11**
Reeve Ct. *Kidd* —3G **11**
Regent M. *B'gve* —4B **22**
Regents Pk. Rd. *B'gve* —2E **23**
Renfrew Gdns. *Kidd* —5C **6**
Reservoir Rd. *Kidd* —1C **10**
Resolution Way. *Stour S* —4B **14**
Reyde Clo. *Redd* —6B **24**
Reynards Clo. *Redd* —5B **24**
Rhuddlan Way. *Kidd* —3E **11**
Ribbesford. —4D 8
Ribbesford Dri. *Stour S* —2G **13**
Ribbesford Rd. *Stour S* —3E **13**
Richmond Rd. *Bew* —6B **4**
Rickyard La. *Redd* —3D **26**
Riddings Clo. *Bew* —5E **5**
Ridgeway, The. *Stour S* —1H **13**
Ridings La. *Redd* —1B **26**
Rifle Range Rd. *Kidd* —1B **10**
Rigby La. *B'gve* —4E **23**
Ringway, The. *Kidd* —4E **7**
Riverside. —3H 25
Riverside. *Stud* —6E **31**
Riverside Cvn. Pk. *Bew* —6C **4**
Riverside Clo. *L End* —4F **19**
Riverside N. *Bew* —6D **4**
Riverway Dri. *Bew* —6D **4**
Road No. 1. *Kidd* —2E **11** (DY10)
Road No. 1. *Kidd* —5C **10** (DY11)
Road No. 3. *Kidd* —2E **11**
Road No. 2. *Kidd* —2E **11** (DY10)
Road No. 2. *Kidd* —5B **10** (DY11)
Robin Ct. *Kidd* —2G **11**
Robins Hill Dri. *A'chu* —5H **21**
Robins La. *Redd* —3C **24**
Rochester Clo. *Head X* —2E **29**
Rochester Wlk. *Kidd* —5H **7**
Rockford Clo. *Redd* —5H **29**
Rock Hill. —5A 22
Rock Hill. *B'gve* —5A **22**
Rockingham Hall Gdns. *Hag* —1H **17**
Rocky La. *B'hth* —2B **18**
Roden Av. *Kidd* —3F **7**
Roman Way. *B'gve* —6E **19**
Romsley Clo. *Redd* —5F **27**
Rookery Clo. *Redd* —1F **29**
Rooks Mdw. *Hag* —2G **17**
Rope Wlk. Bew —6F ***5***
(off Heathfield Rd.)
Rose Av. *A'chu* —4H **21**
Rosedale Clo. *Redd* —3C **24**
Rose Dene. *Stour S* —2G **13**
Rosehall Clo. *Redd* —4G **29**
Rosemary Rd. *Kidd* —3H **7**
Rosenhurst Dri. *Bew* —1C **8**
Rose Ter. *B Grn* —2E **21**
Rosetti Clo. *Kidd* —4H **7**
Rosewood Dri. *B Grn* —3D **20**
Roslin Clo. *B'gve* —3E **23**
Rough Hill Dri. *Redd* —5G **29**
Rough, The. *Head X & Redd* —2F **29**
Rowanberry Clo. *Stour S* —2G **13**
Rowan Clo. *B'gve* —2B **22**
Rowan Cres. *Redd* —4C **24**
Rowan Ho. *Kidd* —1B **6**
Rowan Rd. *Redd* —4C **24**
Rowland Hill Av. *Kidd* —5B **6**
Rowland Hill Cen. Kidd —4E ***7***
(off Worcester St.)
Rowland Way. *Kidd* —3E **11**
Roxall Clo. *Blak* —6B **16**
Roxborough Ho. *Redd* —6F **25**
Royal Sq. *Redd* —5G **25**
Royal Worcester Cres. *B'gve* —2F **23**
Rozel Av. *Kidd* —1H **7**
Runcorn Clo. *Redd* —2H **29**
Rush La. *Redd* —2B **26**
Rushock Clo. *Redd* —3C **30**
Ruskin Av. *Kidd* —4H **7**
Russel Cft. *B'gve* —5D **22**
Russell Rd. *Kidd* —6F **7**
Russett Way. *Bew* —6B **4**
Ruth Chamberlain Ct. Kidd —4D ***6***
(off Paternoster Row)
Rutherford Rd. *B'gve* —6E **23**
Rutland Dri. *B'gve* —4D **22**
Rydal Clo. *Stour S* —6H **9**
Ryefield Clo. *Hag* —4F **17**
Ryegrass La. *Redd* —4E **29**
Ryton Clo. *Redd* —1D **30**
Ryvere Clo. *Stour S* —4H **13**

Sabrina Dri. *Bew* —6C **4**
St Agnes Clo. *Stud* —6C **30**
St Alban's Av. *Kidd* —3A **6**
St Andrews Grn. *Kidd* —6E **7**
St Andrews Way. *B'gve* —4A **22**
St Asaphs Av. *Stud* —6D **30**
St Catherines Clo. *B'wll* —5B **20**
St Catherine's Rd. *B'wll* —4A **20**
St Cecilia Clo. *Kidd* —2E **11**
St Chads Rd. *Stud* —6C **30**
St David's Clo. *Kidd* —4H **5**
St David's Ho. *Redd* —4D **24**
St George's. —4H 25
St Georges Ct. *Kidd* —4F **7**
St Georges Gdns. *Redd* —4H **25**
St George's Pl. *Kidd* —3E **7**
St Georges Rd. *Redd* —4H **25**
St George's Ter. *Kidd* —4F **7**
St Godwald's Cres. *B'gve* —4E **23**
St Godwalds Rd. *B'gve* —5E **23**
St James Ct. B'gve —1D ***22***
(off Strand, The)
St John's Av. *Kidd* —3A **6**
St John's Clo. *Kidd* —4C **6**
St John's Rd. *Stour S* —1A **14**
St John's St. *Kidd* —4C **6**
St John St. *B'gve* —2C **22**
St Judes Av. *Stud* —6C **30**
St Laurence Clo. *A'chu* —1H **21**
St Luke's Cotts. *Redd* —1F **29**
St Martin's Av. *Stud* —6D **30**
St Mary's Ringway. *Kidd* —4D **6**
St Oswalds Clo. *Kidd* —2F **7**
St Patricks Ct. *Kidd* —3B **10**
St Paul's Av. *Kidd* —4A **6**
St Peter's Clo. *Redd* —5G **29**
St Stephen's Gdns. *Redd* —3H **25**
Salford Clo. *Redd* —4B **30**
Salisbury Dri. *Kidd* —4H **5**
Salop Rd. *Redd* —6F **25**
Salter's La. *Redd* —4C **24**
Salwarpe Rd. *B'gve* —4B **22**
Sandbourne Dri. *Bew* —1E **9**
Sanderling Ct. *Kidd* —3G **11**
Sanders Clo. *Redd* —4C **24**
Sanders Ind. Est. *B'gve* —3B **22**
Sanderson Ct. *Kidd* —5C **6**
Sanders Rd. *B'gve* —3B **22**
Sandhills Grn. *B Grn & A'chu* —2F **21**
Sandhills La. *B Grn* —3E **21**
Sandhills Rd. *B Grn* —2E **21**
Sandhurst Clo. *Redd* —2C **26**
Sandicliffe Clo. *Kidd* —2C **6**
Sand Martin Way. *Kidd* —2G **11**
Sandon Clo. *Redd* —5A **26**
Sandown Dri. *Cats* —1E **19**
Sandpiper Clo. *Kidd* —2H **11**
Sandstone Rd. *Bew* —1E **9**
Sandy Bank. *Bew* —1C **8**

Sandygate Clo. *Redd* —6B **24**
Sandy La. *Kidd* —1H **5**
(in two parts)
Sandy La. *Stour S* —5B **14**
Sandy La. Ind. Est. *Stour S*
—6B **14**
Santa Maria Way. *Stour S*
—3B **14**
Santridge Ct. B'gve —6D **18**
(off Bewell Head)
Santridge La. *B'gve* —6D **18**
Sarah Seager Clo. *Stour S*
—6G **9**
Saxon Clo. *Stud* —5E **31**
Scaife Rd. *B'gve* —5E **23**
Scarfield Hill. *A'chu* —5E **21**
School Dri. *Kidd* —2H **21**
School La. *A'chu* —5H **21**
School La. *Hag* —2D **17**
School La. *L End* —4E **19**
Scott Rd. *Redd* —2E **29**
Sculthorpe Rd. *Blak* —6A **16**
Sedgefield Wlk. *Cats* —1E **19**
Sedgley Clo. *Redd* —4H **25**
Seedgreen Clo. *Stour S*
—6G **13**
Selba Dri. *Kidd* —4H **5**
Selsdon Clo. *Kidd* —5B **6**
Serin Clo. *Kidd* —3F **11**
Serpentine, The. *Kidd* —6C **6**
Sevenacres La. *Redd* —3C **26**
Severn Clo. *Cats* —2D **18**
Severn Gro. *Kidd* —1B **10**
Severnhills Dri. *Stour S*
—6F **13**
Severn Quay. *Bew* —1D **8**
Severn Ri. *Stour S* —1G **13**
Severn Rd. *Stour S* —4A **14**
Severn Side. *Stour S* —4A **14**
Severnside Mill. *Bew* —1D **8**
Severn Side N. *Bew* —1D **8**
Severn Side S. *Bew* —1D **8**
Severn Valley Railway.
—5F **7**
(at Kidderminster Town
Station)
Severn Way. *Bew* —2B **8**
Seymour Dri. *Redd* —3A **26**
Seymour Rd. *Kidd* —2B **6**
Shaftesbury Clo. *B'gve*
—2E **23**
Shakespeare Av. *Redd*
—6A **26**
Shakespeare Dri. *Kidd* —4G **7**
Shaw Av. *Kidd* —4H **7**
Shawbank Rd. *Redd* —5B **26**
Shawbury Clo. *Redd* —5E **27**
Shaw Hedge Rd. *Bew* —6E **5**
Shaws Clo. *Redd* —6B **24**
Shearwater Clo. *Kidd* —3H **11**
Sheepcote Grange. *B'gve*
—5C **18**
Sheepcroft Clo. *Redd* —6B **24**
Sheldon Rd. *Redd* —1A **30**
Shelduck Clo. *Kidd* —1H **11**
Shelley Av. *Kidd* —3E **7**
Shelley Clo. *Cats* —2D **18**
Shelley Clo. *Redd* —2E **29**
Sheltwood Clo. *Redd* —6C **24**
Shenstone Clo. *B'gve* —1D **22**
Shenstone Ct. *B'gve* —1E **23**
Shepherds Wlk. *B'gve*
—5B **22**
Shepley Rd. *B Grn* —3B **20**
Sheraton Dri. *Kidd* —4H **7**
Sherbourne Clo. *Redd*
—6D **26**
Sherwood Rd. *B'gve* —5D **22**
Shipston Clo. *Redd* —4C **24**
Shirehampton Clo. *Redd*
—6B **24**
Shireland La. *Redd* —4C **24**
Shrawley Av. *Kidd* —1B **10**
Shrewsbury Rd. *Kidd* —5A **6**
Shrubbery Ct. *Kidd* —3F **7**
Shrubbery Rd. *B'gve* —3B **22**
Shrubbery St. *Kidd* —3F **7**
Sidemoor. —6B 18
Sidings, The. *Stourb* —2F **17**

Sillins Av. *Redd* —5A **26**
Sillins La. *Elc B & Call H*
—4A **28**
Silver Birch Dri. *Kidd* —5H **7**
Silver Birches Bus. Pk. *B'gve*
—6D **22**
Silverdale. *B'gve* —6C **18**
Silverstone Av. *Kidd* —1D **6**
Silver St. *Kidd* —3E **7**
Silver St. *Redd* —5G **25**
Sion Av. *Kidd* —1F **7**
Sion Gdns. *Stour S* —3H **13**
Sion Hill. *Kidd* —1F **7**
Sir George's Mall. *Kidd* —4E **7**
Sir Walters Mall. *Kidd* —4E **7**
Siskin Way. *Kidd* —3H **11**
Skilts Av. *Redd* —1H **29**
Skylark Way. *Kidd* —2G **11**
Slad, The. *Stour S* —6D **10**
Slideslow. —2F 23
Slideslow Av. *B'gve* —2E **23**
Slimbridge Clo. *Redd* —5G **29**
Slough, The. *Redd* —5G **29**
Smallwood. —5H 25
Smallwood Almshouses. *Redd*
—5G **25**
Smallwood St. *Redd* —5G **25**
Smith St. *Redd* —4G **25**
Snake La. *A'chu* —4H **21**
Snakes Lake La. *D'frd* —4A **18**
Snake Ter. *A'chu* —4H **21**
Snowberry Clo. *Stour S*
—2G **13**
Snowdon Clo. *Kidd* —1C **6**
Snowshill Clo. *Redd* —2B **26**
Snuff Mill Wlk. *Bew* —2C **8**
Somerleyton Av. *Kidd* —5G **7**
Somerleyton Ct. *Kidd* —5G **7**
Somerset Dri. *Kidd* —1C **6**
Soudan. *Redd* —6F **25**
Southall Dri. *Hartl* —5G **15**
South Cres. *B'gve* —3D **22**
Southcrest. —6F 25
Southcrest Gdns. *Redd*
—1F **29**
Southcrest Rd. *Redd* —6H **25**
South Gdns. *Hag* —4F **17**
Southgate Clo. *Redd* —6A **6**
Southmead Cres. *Redd*
—5H **25**
Southmead Dri. *L End*
—4E **19**
Southmead Gdns. *Stud*
—6E **31**
S. Moons Moat Ind. Area.
Redd —4D **26**
South Rd. *B'gve* —5E **23**
South Rd. *Hag* —4F **17**
South St. *Redd* —5G **25**
Spadesbourne Rd. *L End*
—4F **19**
Spencer Av. *Bew* —6E **5**
Spencer St. *Kidd* —6C **6**
Spennells. —2G 11
Spennells Valley Rd. *Kidd*
—2F **11**
Spenser Wlk. *Cats* —2D **18**
Spetchley Clo. *Redd* —4E **29**
Spindle Clo. *Kidd* —1D **6**
Spinney Clo. *Kidd* —3A **6**
Spinney M. *Redd* —1E **29**
Spinney Wlk. *Redd* —1E **29**
Spirehouse La. *Burc & B'wll*
—5G **19**
Spire Vw. *B'gve* —1C **22**
Spring Clo. *Hag* —4E **17**
Springfield Av. *B'gve* —5D **22**
Springfield La. *Kidd* —2F **7**
Spring Gro. Cres. *Kidd*
—1B **10**
Spring Gro. Rd. *Kidd* —1B **10**
Springhill Ri. *Bew* —6E **5**
Springs Av. *Cats* —1C **18**
Springside. *Redd* —2B **30**
Springvale Rd. *Redd* —6B **24**
Spruces, The. *Hag* —4E **17**
Square, The. *A'chu* —1H **21**
Stableford Clo. *Redd* —3F **29**
Stable Way. *Stoke H* —6B **22**

Stadium Clo. *Agg* —6F **7**
Stagborough Way. *Stour S*
—1G **13**
Stakenbridge. —5C 16
Stakenbridge La. *C'hll & Hag*
—4B **16**
Stanford Clo. *Redd* —4D **28**
Stanklyn La. *Summ & Stone*
—4G **11**
Stanley Clo. *Redd* —3A **26**
Staple Flat. *L End* —3F **19**
Staple Hill. —2F 19
Stapleton Clo. *Redd* —5D **26**
Stapleton Clo. *Stud* —6D **30**
Stapleton Rd. *Stud* —6D **30**
Station App. *B Grn* —2E **21**
Station App. *Kidd* —5F **7**
Station Cotts. *B'wll* —6B **20**
Station Dri. *Blak* —6B **16**
Station Dri. *Hag* —3F **17**
Station Dri. *Kidd* —5F **7**
Station Rd. *A'chu* —5H **21**
Station Rd. *Bew* —1E **9**
Station Rd. *B'wll* —5B **20**
Station Rd. *Hag* —2F **17**
Station Rd. *Hartl* —4H **15**
Station Rd. *Stud* —6C **30**
Station St. *B'gve* —2C **22**
Station Way. *Redd* —5F **25**
Steatite Way. *Stour S* —1G **13**
Stephenson Pl. *Bew* —1E **9**
Stevenson Av. *Redd* —4H **25**
Stewart Ct. *Kidd* —6F **7**
Stoke Cross. —4G 23
Stoke La. *Redd* —1B **26**
Stoke Rd. *B'gve* —5D **22**
Stokesay Clo. *Redd* —2E **11**
Stonechat Clo. *Kidd* —2H **11**
Stonehouse Clo. *Redd*
—1E **29**
Stonehouse Rd. *B'gve*
—4D **22**
Stoneleigh Clo. *Redd* —1E **29**
Stonepits La. *Redd* —6F **29**
Stoney Hill. —3E 23
Stoney Hill Clo. *B'gve* —3D **22**
Stoney La. *Kidd* —3E **7**
Stoney La. Ind. Est. *Kidd*
—3D **6**
Stourbridge Rd. *Belb* —6E **17**
Stourbridge Rd. *B'gve*
—3C **18**
Stourbridge Rd. *Cats* —1B **18**
Stourbridge Rd. *Hag* —1H **17**
(nr. Birmingham Rd.)
Stourbridge Rd. *Hag* —3H **17**
(nr. Kidderminster Rd.)
Stourbridge Rd. *Kidd & Hurc*
—3E **7**
Stour La. *Stour S* —3A **14**
Stourport Marina. *Stour S*
—6B **14**
Stourport-on-Severn.
—3H **13**
Stourport Rd. *Bew* —1D **8**
Stourport Rd. *Kidd* —4B **10**
Stourport Rd. *Stour S*
—6D **14**
Strand, The. *B'gve* —1D **22**
Stratford Rd. *B'gve* —2D **22**
(in two parts)
Stretton Ho. *Redd* —4C **24**
Stretton Rd. *Kidd* —6B **6**
Stuarts Ct. *Hag* —3F **17**
Studley. —6E 31
Studley Rd. *Redd* —5A **26**
Sugarbrook Rd. *B'gve*
—5D **22**
Sugar Loaf La. *I'ley* —2A **16**
(in two parts)
Summercroft. *Stour S*
—6G **13**
Summercroft. *Stour S*
—6G **13**
Summerfield. —5F 11
Summerfield La. *Summ*
—5F **11**
Summerfield Rd. *Redd*
—2B **14**

Summerhill. —5A 6
Summerhill Av. *Kidd* —4A **6**
Summerhouse Clo. *Call H*
—4C **28**
Summer Pl. *Kidd* —5C **6**
Summer Rd. *Kidd* —1B **10**
Summer St. *Redd* —5G **25**
Summervale Clo. *Hag* —3F **17**
Summervale Rd. *Hag* —3F **17**
Summerway La. *Tort* —6E **11**
Sunningdale. B'gve —3D **22**
(off New Rd.)
Sunningdale Rd. *B'gve*
—4A **22**
Sunnymead. *B'gve* —3D **22**
Sunnyside Gdns. *Kidd* —1B **6**
Sutton Clo. *Redd* —4G **25**
Sutton Farm. —6B 6
Sutton Pk. Gro. *Kidd* —1C **10**
Sutton Pk. Ri. *Kidd* —1A **10**
Sutton Pk. Rd. *Kidd* —6A **6**
Sutton Rd. *Kidd* —5C **6**
Swaledale Clo. *B'gve* —6B **22**
Swallow Dri. *Kidd* —2G **11**
Swan Cen. *Kidd* —4E **7**
Swan Clo. *Blak* —6A **16**
Swan Pas. *Stour S* —3A **14**
Swans Length. *A'chu* —3H **21**
Swan St. *A'chu* —1H **21**
Swans Wlk. *A'chu* —4H **21**
Sweetpool La. *Hag* —1H **17**
Swift Clo. *B'gve* —4B **22**
Swift Pk. Gro. *Kidd* —2H **11**
Swinburne Rd. *Redd* —3E **29**
Swiss Heights. *Stour S*
—5G **13**
Sycamore Av. *Redd* —6G **25**
Sycamore Clo. *Kidd* —3F **7**
Sycamores, The. *Hag* —3E **17**
Sydnall Clo. *Redd* —6B **24**
Sydney Rd. *B'gve* —1B **22**

Tabbs Gdns. *Kidd* —3G **7**
Talbot Clo. *Hartl* —5G **15**
Talbot Rd. *B'gve* —5B **22**
Talbot St. *Kidd* —6C **6**
Tall Trees Clo. *Cats* —2C **18**
Tanglewood Clo. *B'wll*
—4B **20**
Tanhouse La. *Redd* —1C **26**
Tan La. *Stour S* —2H **13**
Tanners Hill. *Bew* —1A **8**
Tanwood Clo. *Call H* —4C **28**
Tanworth La. *Beo* —1H **27**
Tanyard Clo. *A'chu* —1H **21**
Tanyard La. *A'chu* —4H **21**
Tardebigge Ho. B'gve —1E **23**
(off Burcot La.)
Teal Cres. *Kidd* —1G **11**
Teal Rd. *Stour S* —6F **31**
Teeswater Clo. *B'gve* —6B **22**
Telford Dri. *Bew* —1C **8**
Teme Av. *Kidd* —1B **10**
Temple Clo. *Redd* —4H **25**
Tenacres La. *Redd* —5E **27**
Tenbury Clo. *Redd* —2C **26**
Tenby Way. *Stour S* —6G **9**
Tennyson Rd. *Redd* —2E **29**
Tennyson Way. *Kidd* —4H **7**
Terry's Clo. *Redd* —3H **25**
Thames Ho. *Kidd* —2E **11**
Thane Clo. *Stud* —6E **31**
Thicknall La. *Clent* —5E **17**
Thicknall Ri. *Hag* —4F **17**
Thirlmere Rd. *Stour S* —6H **9**
Thirsk Way. *Cats* —1E **19**
Thornbury La. *Redd* —1C **26**
Thorncliffe Clo. *Call H* —4C **28**
Thornhill Rd. *Moons I*
—1E **27**
Throckmorton Rd. *Redd*
—3H **29**
Thruxton Clo. *Redd* —5E **27**
Tibberton Cl. *B'gve* —5B **22**
Ticknall Clo. *Redd* —3C **24**
Tidbury Clo. *Redd* —4E **29**
Tilehouse. *Redd* —6F **25**
Tillington Clo. *Redd* —5E **27**

Timberhonger La. *U War*
—2A **22**
Timber La. *Stour S* —1B **14**
Tintern Clo. *B'gve* —3B **22**
Tintern Clo. *Kidd* —4H **5**
Tipping's Hill. *H End* —5E **29**
Tolley Rd. *Kidd* —3B **10**
Tollhouse Rd. *Stoke H*
—6B **22**
Tomkinson Dri. *Kidd* —6B **6**
Torridon Clo. *Stour S* —5G **9**
Torrs Clo. *Redd* —6F **25**
Torton. —1H 15
Torton La. *Tort* —1H **15**
Towbury Clo. *Redd* —5H **29**
Tower Bldgs. *Kidd* —4C **7**
Tower Dri. *B'gve* —4D **18**
Tower Rd. *Kidd* —5H **7**
Townsend Av. *B'gve* —6E **19**
Trafford Pk., The. *Redd*
—5H **25**
Tram St. *Kidd* —5E **7**
Tranter Av. *A'chu* —5H **21**
Tredington Clo. *Redd* —4B **30**
Trescott Rd. *Redd* —5H **25**
Treville Clo. *Redd* —5E **27**
Trevithick Clo. *Stour S*
—2A **14**
Trickses La. *Ham G* —6A **28**
Trimpley. —1E 5
Trimpley Dri. *Kidd* —3A **6**
Trimpley La. *Bew* —5F **5**
Trimpley Rd. *Trim & Low H*
—1E **5**
Trinity Clo. *B'gve* —5E **23**
Trinity Clo. *Kidd* —4G **7**
Trinity Fields. *Kidd* —4F **7**
Trinity Grange. *Kidd* —3F **7**
Truro Dri. *Redd* —4A **6**
Tryst, The. *B'gve* —5E **19**
Tudor Rd. *Bew* —1B **8**
Tunnel Dri. *Redd* —6G **25**
Turnpike La. *Redd* —4C **24**
Turnstone Rd. *Kidd* —3G **11**
Turton St. *Kidd* —2G **7**
Twatling Rd. *B Grn* —1B **20**
Twiners Rd. *Redd* —1H **29**
Tynes, The. *Stoke H* —5B **22**
Tynings Clo. *Kidd* —1B **6**
Tynsall Av. *Redd* —6B **24**
Tysoe Clo. *Redd* —6D **26**
Tythe Barn Clo. *Stoke H*
—6A **22**

Ullapool Clo. *H End* —4F **29**
Ullenhall La. *Beo* —2H **27**
Ullswater Av. *Stour S* —6H **9**
Underhill Clo. *Redd* —4H **29**
Underwood Clo. *Call H*
—3C **28**
Unicorn Hill. *Redd* —4F **25**
Union St. *Kidd* —3E **7**
Union St. *Redd* —5H **25**
Upland Gro. *B'gve* —5D **18**
Upland Rd. *B'gve* —6D **18**
Upleadon Clo. *Call H* —4C **28**
Upper Catshill. —1E 19
Up. Crossgate Rd. *Park I*
—2C **30**
Up. Field Clo. *Redd* —2C **24**
Up. Gambolds La. *S Prior*
—6F **23**
Upper Marlbrook. —1G 19
Upton Clo. *Redd* —5F **27**
Upton Rd. *Kidd* —1F **7**
Usmere Rd. *Kidd* —5C **6**
Uxbridge Ct. *Kidd* —5C **6**

Vale Ind. Est. *Kidd* —3C **10**
Vale Rd. *Stour S* —3A **14**
Valley Clo. *Call H* —4C **28**
Valley Gro. *Low H* —2G **5**
Valley Rd. *B'hth* —3B **18**
Valley Vw. *Bew* —2B **8**
Vawdrey Clo. *Stour S* —5G **13**

Vaynor Dri. *Redd* —2F **29**
Venus Bank. *Bew* —1C **8**
Vernon Clo. *Redd* —3A **26**
Vernon Rd. *Stour S* —2A **14**
Vicarage Clo. *B'gve* —4E **23**
Vicarage Cres. *Kidd* —5F **7**
Vicarage Cres. *Redd* —5E **25**
(in two parts)
Vicarage Vw. *Redd* —5F **25**
Vicar St. *Kidd* —4E **7**
Victoria Ct. *Kidd* —4F **7**
Victoria M. *B Grn* —2E **21**
Victoria Pl. *Kidd* —1B **10**
Victoria St. *Redd* —4G **25**
Victory Clo. *Stour S* —4B **14**
Village, The. —4F **15**
Villiers Rd. *B'gve* —5A **22**
Villiers St. *Kidd* —5G **7**
Vine St. *Kidd* —2G **7**
Vine St. *Redd* —4F **25**
Vowchurch Clo. *Redd* —3C **24**

Wadey Pl. *Bew* —5F **5**
Waggoners Clo. *Stoke H*
—6B **22**
Waggon La. *Kidd* —5A **16**
Walford Wlk. *Redd* —5G **25**
Walker Dri. *Kidd* —1G **7**
Walkers Rd. *Moons I* —2E **27**
Walkwood. —5D **28**
Walkwood Cres. *Redd*
—4E **29**
Walkwood Rd. *Redd* —4E **29**
Wallhouse La. *Elc B* —5A **28**
Walnut La. *Fins* —4G **23**
Walshes, The. —5G **13**
Walter Nash Rd. E. *Kidd*
—3A **10**
Walter Nash Rd. W. *Kidd*
—3A **10**
Waltham Clo. *B'gve* —3B **22**
Walton Clo. *Kidd* —2B **10**
Walton Clo. *Redd* —5E **27**
Walton Clo. *Stour S* —5F **13**
Walton La. *Hartl* —4H **15**
Walton Rd. *B'gve* —6D **18**
Wannerton Rd. *Blak* —6A **16**
Wapping. —2H **27**
(nr. Moons Moat)
Wapping. —5D **30**
(nr. Studley)
Wapping La. *Beo* —1H **27**
Warbank Clo. *A'chu* —4H **21**
Warbler Pl. *Kidd* —2G **11**
Waresley. —6G **15**
Waresley Ct. Rd. *Hartl*
—5G **15**
Waresley Park. —5G **15**
Waresley Rd. *Hartl* —5G **15**
Warstone Clo. *Bew* —6F **5**
Warwick Av. *B'gve* —5D **22**
Warwick Clo. *Stud* —6D **30**
Warwick Hall Gdns. *B'gve*
—4D **22**
Warwick Highway. *Map G &
Stud* —1H **29**
Warwick St. *Stour S* —1A **14**
Washford. —3E **31**
Washford Dri. *Park I* —3C **30**
Washford Ind. Est. *Redd*
—2E **31**

Washford La. *Redd* —2D **30**
Washington St. *Kidd* —5C **6**
Wassell Dri. *Bew* —6E **5**
Wassell Wood
Nature Reserve. —3F **5**
Watchtower Rd. *Stour S*
—6D **10**
Waterlaide Clo. *Hartl* —4H **15**
Waterlaide Rd. *Hartl* —4G **15**
Waterloo Rd. *Bew* —2B **8**
Waterloo St. *Kidd* —4E **7**
Watery La. *Redd* —1A **30**
Watery La. *Stour S* —5A **14**
Watt Clo. *B'gve* —3C **22**
Watt Ct. *Stour S* —5A **14**
Waverley Clo. *Kidd* —2F **7**
Way Cft. *Kidd* —4A **10**
Weatheroak Clo. *Redd*
—1C **28**
Weavers Hill. *H End* —6F **29**
Webheath. —6C 24
*Weethley Ho. Redd —4C 24
(off Lock Clo.)*
Weights La. *Redd* —1D **24**
Welbeck Dri. *Kidd* —5B **6**
Welch Ga. *Bew* —1C **8**
Welcome Dri. *Cats* —1D **18**
Welford Clo. *Redd* —5H **29**
Well Clo. *Redd* —5G **29**
Wellesbourne Clo. *Redd*
—4G **25**
Wellington Ct. *Kidd* —5C **6**
Wellington Rd. *B'gve* —4D **22**
Wellington St. *Redd* —4G **25**
Well La. *B'gve* —2D **22**
Wendron Clo. *B'gve* —2E **23**
Wenlock Dri. *B'gve* —5D **18**
Wenlock Way. *Stour S*
—5G **13**
Wentworth Dri. *B'wll* —5B **20**
Wesley Av. *Stour S* —5G **13**
Wesley Wlk. *Stour S* —5B **22**
West Av. *Redd* —5G **25**
Westbourne Clo. *B'gve*
—3B **22**
Westbourne St. *Bew* —1D **8**
Westbourne Ter. *B'gve*
—3B **22**
West Ct. *S Prior* —6C **22**
Western Rd. *Hag* —4F **17**
Western Way. *Kidd* —5A **6**
Westfields. *Cats* —2C **18**
West Hagley. —3E 17
West Midlands Safari &
Leisure Pk. —1G **9**
Westminster Clo. *B'gve*
—3A **22**
Westminster Ct. *B'gve*
—2D **22**
Westminster Rd. *Kidd* —4H **5**
West Rd. *B'gve* —3D **22**
West St. *Redd* —5G **25**
Westville Av. *Stour S* —5A **6**
Wharrington Clo. *Redd*
—2A **30**
Wharrington Hill. *Redd*
—2A **30**
Wheatmill Clo. *Blak* —6A **16**
Wheatridge Rd. *Stoke H*
—6A **22**
Wheelers La. *Redd* —3C **24**

Wheeley Rd. *A'chu* —6D **20**
Wheelwright Clo. *B'gve*
—6B **22**
Whimbrel Gro. *Kidd* —3G **11**
Whinchat Gro. *Kidd* —2G **11**
Whitburn Clo. *Kidd* —5B **6**
Whitchurch Clo. *Redd*
—4H **29**
Whitegate Dri. *Kidd* —1A **10**
White Heart Clo. *Bew* —1B **8**
Whitehill Rd. *Kidd* —1H **9**
White Ho. Dri. *B Grn* —1B **20**
Whitehouse La. *Redd* —5E **27**
Whitehouse Rd. *Kidd* —6D **6**
Whitford Clo. *B'gve* —3A **22**
Whitford Gdns. *B'gve* —2A **22**
Whitford Rd. *B'gve* —2A **22**
(in two parts)
Whitlenge La. *Hartl* —4H **15**
Whittall Dri. E. *Kidd* —3B **10**
Whittall Dri. W. *Kidd* —3A **10**
Whitville Clo. *Kidd* —3C **6**
Wickham La. *Stud* —6F **31**
Wilden. —6D 10
Wilden Ind. Est. *Stour S*
—6C **10**
Wilden La. *Stour S* —2C **14**
Wilden Top Rd. *Stour S*
—2D **14**
Wild Goose La. *Redd* —1D **30**
Wildmoor La. *Cats* —1D **18**
William Bullock Clo. *Stour S*
—3H **13**
William Coley Pl. *Stour S*
—5H **13**
William St. *Redd* —4G **25**
Willis St. *Kidd* —5G **7**
Willow Brook Rd. *A'chu*
—3H **21**
Willow Clo. *B'gve* —2B **22**
Willow Clo. *Hag* —3E **17**
Willow Ct. *B'gve* —1B **22**
Willowdene. *Stour S* —3B **14**
Willowfield Dri. *Kidd* —2C **6**
Willow Gdns. *B'gve* —1B **22**
Willow Rd. *B'gve* —1B **22**
Willows, The. *Stour S* —2C **14**
Willow Tree Dri. *B Grn*
—2E **21**
Willow Way. *Redd* —4D **24**
Wilmcote Ct. *B'gve* —4A **22**
*Wilmcote Ho. Redd —4C 24
(off Cardy Clo.)*
Wilson Rd. *Hartl* —5G **15**
Wilton Av. *Kidd* —3A **6**
(in two parts)
Winbrook. *Bew* —1C **8**
Winchester Av. *Kidd* —4A **6**
Winchester Clo. *Hag* —2F **17**
Windermere Ho. *Kidd* —3E **7**
Windermere Way. *Stour S*
—6G **9**
Windmill Clo. *Stour S* —5H **13**
Windmill Dri. *Redd* —4E **29**
Windmill La. *Call H* —4D **28**
Windrush Clo. *Redd* —4F **29**
Windsor Dri. *Kidd* —3E **7**
Windsor Dri. *Stour S* —6H **13**
Windsor Gdns. *B'gve* —2D **22**
Windsor Rd. *Redd* —3F **25**
Windsor St. *B'gve* —2C **22**
Windsor St. *Redd* —4F **25**
Winds Point. *Hag* —2F **17**

Winforton Clo. *Redd* —5E **27**
Winslow Clo. *Redd* —5F **27**
Winstone Clo. *Redd* —4A **26**
Winterfold Clo. *Kidd* —4H **7**
Wintour Wlk. *B'gve* —5B **22**
Winward Rd. *Redd* —1F **31**
Winyate Hill. *Redd* —6A **26**
Winyates. —4D 26
Winyates Green. —5F 27
Winyates Way. *Redd* —3E **27**
Wirehill Dri. *Redd* —1H **29**
Wishaw Clo. *Redd* —2A **30**
Withybed Clo. *A'chu* —4H **21**
Withybed Green. —4G 21
Withybed La. *A'chu* —4G **21**
Witley Clo. *Kidd* —2B **10**
Witley Way. *Stour S* —6F **13**
Wiveldem Av. *Stour S* —6D **10**
Woburn Clo. *B'gve* —3A **22**
Wolverhampton Rd. *Redd*
—1G **7**
Wolverley Rd. *Kidd* —1B **6**
Wolverton Clo. *Redd* —6D **26**
Woodbank Dri. *Cats* —2C **18**
Woodberrow La. *Redd*
—4F **29**
Woodbury Clo. *Call H* —4C **28**
Woodbury Clo. *Hartl* —5G **15**
Woodbury Dri. *B Grn* —1B **20**
Woodbury Rd. *Kidd* —2B **10**
Woodbury Rd. *Stour S*
—1H **13**
Woodbury Rd. N. *Stour S*
—1H **13**
Woodbury Rd. W. *Stour S*
—1H **13**
Woodchester. *Hag* —4G **17**
Woodcote Clo. *Redd* —5E **27**
Wood Ct. *Redd* —1E **29**
Woodcroft Clo. *B'wll* —5A **20**
Woodend Clo. *Redd* —6D **24**
Wood End Dri. *B Grn* —2B **20**
Woodfield Clo. *Redd* —3A **26**
Woodfield Cres. *Kidd* —5C **6**
Woodfield St. *Kidd* —4C **6**
Woodgate Ho. *Redd* —4C **24**
Woodgreen Clo. *Call H*
—3D **28**
Woodhampton Clo. *Stour S*
—6H **13**
Woodland Av. *Hag* —3E **17**
Woodland Av. *Kidd* —3C **6**
Woodland Rd. *Redd* —5D **24**
Woodlands Clo. *Hartl* —4H **15**
Woodlands, The. *Kidd*
—1B **10**
Woodpecker Gro. *Kidd*
—2H **11**
Wood Piece La. *Redd* —1D **26**
Woodrow. —3B 30
Woodrow. *Redd* —3A **30**
Woodrow Cen. *Redd* —2B **30**
(in two parts)
Woodrow Clo. *Cats* —1C **18**
Woodrow La. *Cats* —1D **18**
Woodrow N. *Redd* —3A **30**
Woodrow Shop. Cen. *Redd*
—3B **30**
Woodrow S. *Redd* —3B **30**
Woodside Av. *Redd* —6D **24**
Wood Side Dri. *B Grn* —2C **20**
Wood St. *Kidd* —4D **6**

Woodthorpe Dri. *Bew* —6C **4**
Woodward Rd. *Kidd* —1C **10**
Woolaston Rd. *Redd* —2C **30**
Woolhope Clo. *Redd* —5E **27**
Wooton Clo. *Redd* —4C **24**
Worcester Clo. *Hag* —3F **17**
*Worcester Cross. Kidd —5E 7
(off Ringway, The)*
Worcester La. *Hag* —1G **17**
Worcester Rd. *B'gve* —4B **22**
Worcester Rd. *Hag* —5E **17**
Worcester Rd. *Kidd* —5E **7**
(nr. Marlborough St.)
Worcester Rd. *Kidd* —6E **7**
(nr. Ringway, The)
Worcester Rd. *Shen* —6H **11**
Worcester Rd. *Stoke H*
—6A **22**
Worcester Rd. *Stour S*
—3B **14**
Worcester Rd. *Summ & Hartl*
—4G **11**
Worcester Sq. *Redd* —4G **25**
Worcester St. *Kidd* —4E **7**
Worcester St. *Stour S* —2A **14**
Wordsley Clo. *Redd* —1B **26**
Wordsworth Av. *Redd* —2E **29**
Wordsworth Cres. *Kidd*
—4H **7**
Worms Ash. —4A 18
Worth Cres. *Stour S* —6F **9**
Wrekin Clo. *Kidd* —2B **10**
Wrekin Dri. *B'gve* —5D **18**
Wrekin Wlk. *Stour S* —5F **13**
Wribbenhall. —1E 9
Wychbold Clo. *Call H* —4C **28**
Wychbold Ct. *Stourb* —1H **17**
Wychbury Dri. *Hag* —1H **17**
Wychwood Dri. *Redd* —4F **29**
Wynn Clo. *Bew* —5F **5**
Wyre Hill. *Bew* —2A **8**

Yardley Clo. *Redd* —5E **27**
Yarningale Clo. *Redd* —4H **29**
Yarnold La. *B'hth* —1A **18**
Yarranton Clo. *Stour S*
—6G **13**
Yeadon Clo. *Redd* —1C **28**
Yellowhammer Ct. *Kidd*
—3G **11**
Yeoman Clo. *Kidd* —1E **11**
Yeomans Wlk. *B'gve* —4C **22**
Yew Tree Clo. *Bew* —1B **8**
Yew Tree Clo. *Redd* —4C **24**
Yew Tree Clo. *Stour S*
—2G **13**
Yew Tree Dri. *B'gve* —2E **23**
Yew Tree La. *Bew* —1B **8**
Yew Tree Rd. *Kidd* —5F **7**
York Av. *B'gve* —6B **18**
York Clo. *B'gve* —6B **18**
York Clo. *Stud* —6C **30**
York Rd. *Bew* —6B **4**
York Rd. *B'gve* —6B **18**
York St. *Kidd* —3E **7**
York St. *Stour S* —3A **14**
Yvonne Rd. *Redd* —4E **29**

Zortech Av. *Kidd* —4A **10**

Other A-Z Publications

A-Z STREET ATLASES

Aldershot ■ Bangor ■ Barnet ■ Barnsley ■ Basingstoke ■ Birmingham ■ Birmingham Mini ■ Birmingham De Luxe ■ Blackburn/Burnley ■ Blackpool ■ Bolton ■ Bournemouth ■ Bracknell ■ Bradford ■ Brighton/Worthing ■ Bristol / Bath ■ Bristol / Bath Deluxe ■ Bromley ■ Burton upon Trent ■ Bury ■ Cambridge ■ Cannock ■ Cardiff/Newport ■ Chelmsford ■ Cheltenham/Gloucester/Stroud ■ Chester ■ Chesterfield ■ Chichester/Bognor Regis ■ Colchester ■ Coventry/Rugby ■ Crawley ■ Croydon ■ Darlington ■ Dartford ■ Derby ■ Doncaster ■ Durham ■ Eastbourne ■ Edinburgh ■ Exeter ■ Folkestone/Dover ■ Glasgow ■ Glasgow De Luxe ■ Guildford / Woking ■ Hamilton/Motherwell ■ Harlow ■ Harrow ■ Hatfield ■ Hayes ■ Hemel Hempstead ■ Huddersfield ■ Ipswich ■ Lancaster ■ Leeds ■ Leeds/Bradford ■ Leicester ■ Lincoln ■ Liverpool ■ Liverpool De Luxe ■ London ■ "Big" London ■ London Large Format ■ London Mini ■ Inner London & Docklands ■ Geographers' London Atlas (Spiral & Cased) ■ Master Atlas of Greater London (Paper & Cased) ■ London Motorists' Atlas ■ Loughborough ■ Luton / Dunstable ■ Macclesfield ■ Maidstone / Chatham ■ Manchester ■ Manchester De Luxe ■ Manchester Mini ■ Mansfield ■ Margate / Ramsgate ■ Middlesbrough/Stockton ■ Milton Keynes ■ Newbury ■ Newcastle upon Tyne / Sunderland / Durham ■ Northampton ■ Norwich ■ Nottingham ■ Nottingham/Derby ■ Nuneaton ■ Oldham/Rochdale ■ Oxford ■ Paisley ■ Peterborough ■ Plymouth ■ Portsmouth ■ Portsmouth/Southampton ■ Preston ■ Reading ■ Redditch ■ Reigate/Redhill ■ Richmond/Kingston upon Thames ■ Romford ■ Rotherham ■ Royal Tunbridge Wells / Tonbridge ■ St. Albans ■ St. Helens ■ Sheffield ■ Slough ■ Southampton ■ Southampton/Portsmouth/Winchester ■ Southend ■ Southport ■ Stafford ■ Staines ■ Stratford-upon-Avon ■ Stevenage ■ Stockport ■ Stoke-on-Trent ■ Swansea ■ Swindon ■ Taunton ■ Torbay ■ Wakefield ■ Warrington ■ Watford ■ Weymouth / Dorchester ■ Wigan ■ Winchester ■ Wirral ■

A-Z STREET PLANS

Coloured ■
Black & White ❏

Barnet ❏ Bath ■ Bexley ❏ Blackburn ■ Blackpool ■ Bournemouth ■ Cambridge ■ Canterbury ■ Cheltenham ■ Chester ■ Coventry ■ Croydon ❏ Darlington ■ Durham ■ Exeter ■ Gloucester ■ Harrow ❏ Hartlepool ■ Hayes ❏ Hounslow ❏ Ilford/Romford ❏ Lancaster ■ Lincoln ■ Milton Keynes ■ Northampton ■ Norwich ■ Oxford ■ Peterborough ■ Portsmouth ■ Preston ■ Reading ■ Slough ■ Southampton ■ Staines ❏ Stoke-on-Trent ❏ Stratford-upon-Avon ■ Sutton/Epsom ❏ Swansea ■ Swindon ■ Taunton ■ Torbay ■ Walton-on-Thames ❏ Warrington ■ Watford ❏ Wolverhampton ■

A-Z ROAD ATLASES

■ Great Britain Road Atlas (Flexibound & Spiral)
■ G.B. Road Atlas Super Scale/Spiral Bound
■ G.B. Road Atlas Large Format
■ Handy G.B. Road Atlas ■ Mini G.B.Road Atlas

Regional Atlases
South East England ■ Southern England ■ East Anglia ■ Wales ■ Devon & Cornwall Visitors' Atlas ■ Scotland Visitors' Atlas ■ Isle of Wight Visitors' Atlas ■ London Motorists' Atlas ■

A-Z ROAD & COUNTY MAPS

■ A-Z Gt. Britain Road Map Series:(5 miles to 1inch)
✳ S.E. and Central England ✳ S.W. England and S. Wales ✳ Wales and Central England ✳ Northern England ✳ Scotland (Reversible)
■ A-Z Gt. Britain Road Map Series: (3 miles to 1inch)
1. Devon and Cornwall **2.** Southern England **3.** London Home Counties **4.** 50 Miles Around Bristol **5.** South Wales **6.** 50 Miles Around Birmingham **7.** East Anglia **8.** North Wales **9.** 50 Miles Around Manchester/Liverpool **10.** East Midlands **11.** Yorkshire and Humberside **12.** 50 Miles Around Newcastle upon Tyne **13.** Central Scotland
■ Great Britain Road Map (Reversible)
■ Great Britain Road Map
■ Motorways Map: England and Wales M25 / London (Reversible)
■ G.B. Counties & Unitary Authorities Map
■ 50 Miles Around London
■ 35 Miles Around London ✳ London to the South East Coast ✳ London to the South Coast ✳ Cotswolds & Chilterns ✳ Hampshire / Dorset / Wilts ✳ Kent County ✳ Surrey ✳ East Sussex / West Sussex ✳
■ Visitors' Maps of: Devon ✳ Cornwall ✳ Isle of Wight ✳ Lake District ✳ Peak District ✳

A-Z COUNTY STREET ATLASES

Berkshire ■ Essex ■ Greater Manchester ■ Hampshire ■ Hertfordshire ■ Kent ■ Lancashire (Spiral & Cased) ■ Merseyside ■ Surrey (Flexibound & Spiral) ■ South Yorkshire ■ Tyne & Wear ■ West Midlands ■ West Yorkshire ■

A-Z CITY & TOWN MAPS

■ *Premier Street Map Series:* Birmingham ✳ Bradford ✳ Bristol ✳ Cardiff ✳ Derby ✳ Edinburgh ✳ Glasgow ✳ Leeds ✳ Leicester ✳ Liverpool ✳ London ✳ Manchester ✳ Middlesbrough ✳ Newcastle uponTyne ✳ Nottingham ✳ Plymouth ✳ Sheffield ✳ Sunderland ✳

■ *Other London Publications:* Greater London on CD ROM ✳ Main Road London ✳ 9 Sheet Master Maps of London ✳ 6" Map of Central London ✳ 9" Super Scale Map ✳ Visitors' London Atlas and Guide ✳ Visitors' London ✳ Handy Map of Central London ✳ Administrative Boundaries & Postcode Map of London ✳ London Map and Walks ✳Tourists' London Map/Guide

A-Z MINI MAPS

Birmingham ■ Cambridge ■ Coventry ■ Edinburgh ■ Leeds ■ Liverpool ■ London West End ■ Manchester ■ Newcastle ■ Norwich ■ Nottingham ■ Oxford ■ Portsmouth ■ Sheffield ■ Southampton ■

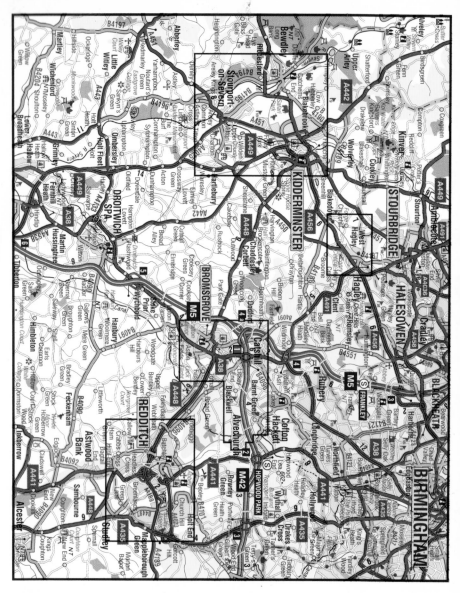

A-Z maps online @
www.a-zmaps.co.uk®

Geographers' A-Z Map Company Ltd

Head Office : (General Enquiries & Trade Sales)
Fairfield Road, Borough Green, Sevenoaks,
Kent TN15 8PP Telephone: 01732 781000

Showrooms : (Retail Sales)
44 Gray's Inn Road, London, WC1X 8HX
Telephone: 020 7440 9500

A-Z AZ AtoZ
registered trade marks of
Geographers' A-Z Map Company Ltd

ISBN 0-85039-911-4

9 780850 399110

£3.25

Monika Schraft

Die Entstehung von Lebensstilen

Studienarbeit